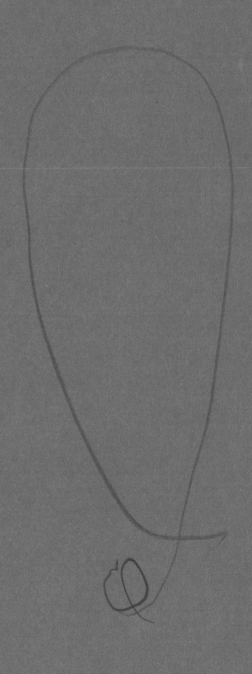

VOICES
for Democracy

Literacy empowers us to be part of the democratic process.

SCHOLASTIC
LITERACY
PLACE®

Copyright acknowledgments and credits appear on page 144, which constitutes an extension of this copyright page.

Copyright © 1996 by Scholastic Inc.   All rights reserved.   Printed in the U.S.A.
ISBN 0-590-49193-8

4 5 6 7 8 9 10   24   02 01 00 99 98 97

Learn

About a Courthouse

Literacy empowers us to be part of the democratic process.

Justice for All

Democracy provides a system to resolve issues.

CALIFORNIA
VEHICLE CODE NO. 21212
OPERATION OF BICYCLES

(a) A person under 18 years of age shall not operate a bicycle, or ride upon a bicycle as a passenger, upon a street, bikeway, or any other public bicycle path or trail unless that person is wearing a properly fitted and fastened bicycle helmet that meets the standards of the American National Standards Institute... This requirement also applies to a person who rides upon a bicycle while in a restraining seat that is attached to the bicycle or in a trailer towed by the bicycle.

(b) Any helmet sold or offered for sale for use by operators and passengers of bicycles shall be conspicuously labeled in accordance with the standard described in (a).

(c) No person shall sell or offer for sale for use by an operator or passenger of a bicycle any safety helmet which is not of a type meeting requirements.

The Power of Words

Communication advances the democratic process.

Are tests a good measure of what you have learned?

POINT

Amie F. "I think tests accurately measure what I've learned. Teachers can tell what you have learned and what you haven't learned from tests. After they grade the test, teachers can go back and teach you more about...

COUNTERPOINT

Leslie M. "I don't think tests are a good measure of what you've learned. Kids jam everything into their heads before a test to try to do well. But during the test or after the test th...

Taking a Stand

In a democracy, people are empowered to voice their concern for others.

Trade Books

The following books accompany this *Voices for Democracy* SourceBook.

Nonfiction

The Day the Women Got the Vote

by George Sullivan

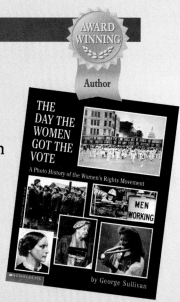

Biography

Nelson Mandela

by Barry Denenberg

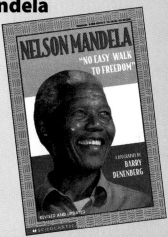

Biography

Thurgood Marshall, Champion of Justice

by G.S. Prentzas

Newbery Honor

Novel

The True Confessions of Charlotte Doyle

by Avi

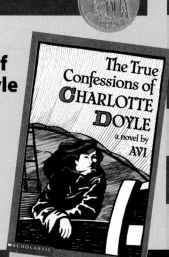

Justice for All

Laugh with Alice as she watches the absurd trial of the Knave of Hearts. See if you can figure out who is telling the truth in a puzzling case.

Meet Judge Mary Ann Vial Lemmon, who has made working for justice her profession. Then read three tales about justice.

WORKSHOP 1

Protect your rights and the rights of others by writing a law.

CALIFORNIA
VEHICLE CODE NO. 21212
OPERATION OF BICYCLES

from # Alice in Wonderland

by *Lewis Carroll*
illustrated by John Tenniel

In 1864, Alice in Wonderland *appeared in the bookstores.
The fantasy, about a girl named Alice who fell down a rabbit hole and into a strange
and absurd world, quickly became a classic. Alice has many adventures involving
a talking rabbit, a grinning Cheshire cat, and the fact that she keeps growing and
shrinking in size. But one of the strangest adventures of all was the trial of the
Knave of Hearts, presided over by the King and Queen of Hearts.*

Who Stole the Tarts?

The King and Queen of Hearts were seated on their throne when they arrived, with a great crowd assembled about them—all sorts of little birds and beasts, as well as the whole pack of cards; the Knave was standing before them, in chains, with a soldier on each side to guard him; and near the King was the White Rabbit, with a trumpet in one hand, and a scroll of parchment in the other. In the very middle of the court was a table, with a large dish of tarts upon it; they looked so good that it made Alice quite hungry to look at them. "I wish they'd get the trial done," she thought, "and hand round the refreshments!" But there seemed to be no chance of this, so she began looking at everything about her, to pass away the time.

Alice had never been in a court of justice before, but she had read about them in books, and she was quite pleased to find that she knew the name of nearly everything there. "That's the judge," she said to herself, "because of his great wig."

The judge, by the way, was the King, and as he wore his crown over the wig, he did not look at all comfortable, and it was certainly not becoming.

"And that's the jury box," thought Alice, "and those twelve creatures" (she was obliged to say "creatures," you see, because some of them were animals, and some were birds), "I suppose they are the jurors." She said this last word two or three times over to herself, being rather proud of it; for she thought, and rightly too, that very few little girls of her age knew the meaning of it at all. However, "jurymen" would have done just as well.

The twelve jurors were all writing very busily on slates. "What are they doing?" Alice whispered to the Gryphon. "They can't have anything to put down yet, before the trial's begun."

"They're putting down their names," the Gryphon whispered in reply, "for fear they should forget them before the end of the trial."

"Stupid things!" Alice began in a loud, indignant voice, but she stopped herself hastily, for the White Rabbit cried out, "Silence in the court!" and the King put on his spectacles and looked anxiously round, to make out who was talking.

Alice could see, as well as if she were looking over their shoulders, that all the jurors were writing down "stupid things!" on their slates, and she could even make out that one of them didn't know how to spell "stupid," and that he had to ask his neighbor to tell him. "A nice muddle their slates'll be in before the trial's over!" thought Alice.

One of the jurors had a pencil that squeaked. This, of course, Alice could *not* stand, and she went round the court and got behind him, and very soon found an opportunity of taking it away. She did it so quickly that the poor little juror (it was Bill, the Lizard) could not make out at all what had become of it; so, after hunting all about for it, he was obliged to write with one finger for the rest of the day; and this was of very little use, as it left no mark on the slate.

"Herald, read the accusation!" said the King.

On this the White Rabbit blew three blasts on the trumpet, and then unrolled the parchment scroll, and read as follows:

> *"The Queen of Hearts, she made some tarts,*
>   *All on a summer day:*
> *The Knave of Hearts, he stole those tarts,*
>   *And took them quite away!"*

"Consider your verdict," the King said to the jury.

"Not yet, not yet!" the Rabbit hastily interrupted. "There's a great deal to come before that!"

"Call the first witness," said the King; and the White Rabbit blew three blasts on the trumpet, and called out, "First witness!"

The first witness was the Hatter. He came in with a teacup in one hand, and a piece of bread and butter in the other. "I beg pardon, your Majesty," he began, "for bringing these in; but I hadn't quite finished my tea when I was sent for."

"You ought to have finished," said the King. "When did you begin?"

The Hatter looked at the March Hare, who had followed

him into the court, arm in arm with the Dormouse. "Four-teenth of March, I *think* it was," he said.

"Fifteenth," said the March Hare.

"Sixteenth," added the Dormouse.

"Write that down," the King said to the jury, and the jury eagerly wrote down all three dates on their slates, and then added them up, and reduced the answer to shillings and pence.

"Take off your hat," the King said to the Hatter.

"It isn't mine," said the Hatter.

"Stolen!" the King exclaimed, turning to the jury, who instantly made a memorandum of the fact.

"I keep them to sell," the Hatter added as an explanation. "I've none of my own. I'm a hatter."

Here the Queen put on her spectacles, and began staring hard at the Hatter, who turned pale and fidgeted.

"Give your evidence," said the King, "and don't be nervous, or I'll have you executed on the spot."

This did not seem to encourage the witness at all; he kept shifting from one foot to the other, looking uneasily at the Queen, and in his confusion he bit a large piece out of his teacup instead of the bread and butter.

Just at this moment Alice felt a very curious sensation, which puzzled her a good deal until she made out what it was; she was beginning to grow larger again; and she thought at first she would get up and leave the court; but on second thought she decided to remain where she was as long as there was room for her.

"I wish you wouldn't squeeze so," said the Dormouse, who was sitting next to her. "I can hardly breathe."

"I can't help it," said Alice very meekly; "I'm growing."

"You've no right to grow *here,*" said the Dormouse.

"Don't talk nonsense," said Alice more boldly; "you know you're growing too."

"Yes, but *I* grow at a reasonable pace," said the Dormouse, "not in that ridiculous fashion." And he got up very sulkily and crossed over to the other side of the court.

All this time the Queen had never left off staring at the Hatter, and, just as the Dormouse crossed the court, she said to one of the officers of the court, "Bring me the list of the singers in the last concert!" On which the wretched Hatter trembled so that he shook both his shoes off.

"Give your evidence," the King repeated angrily, "or I'll have you executed, whether you're nervous or not."

"I'm a poor man, your Majesty," the Hatter began in a trembling voice, "and I hadn't but just begun my tea—not above a week or so—and what with the bread and butter getting so thin—and the twinkling of the tea—"

"The twinkling of *what?*" said the King.

"It *began* with the tea," the Hatter replied.

"Of course twinkling begins with a T!" said the King sharply. "Do you take me for a dunce? Go on!"

"I'm a poor man," the Hatter went on, "and most things twinkled after that—only the March Hare said—"

"I didn't!" the March Hare interrupted in a great hurry.

"You did!" said the Hatter.

"I deny it!" said the March Hare.

"He denies it," said the King; "leave out that part."

"Well, at any rate, the Dormouse said—" the Hatter went on, looking anxiously round to see if he would deny it too; but the Dormouse denied nothing, being fast asleep.

"After that," continued the Hatter, "I cut some more bread and butter—"

"But what did the Dormouse say?" one of the jury asked.

"That I can't remember," said the Hatter.

"You *must* remember," remarked the King, "or I'll have you executed."

The miserable Hatter dropped his teacup and bread and butter, and went down on one knee. "I'm a poor man, your Majesty," he began.

"You're a *very* poor *speaker*," said the King.

Here one of the guinea pigs cheered, and was immediately suppressed by the officers of the court. (As that is rather a hard word, I will just explain to you how it was done. They had a large canvas bag, which tied up at the mouth with strings; into this they slipped the guinea pig, head first, and then sat upon it.)

"I'm glad I've seen that done," thought Alice. "I've so often read in the newspapers, at the end of trials, 'There was some attempt at applause, which was immediately suppressed by the officers of the court,' and I never understood what it meant till now."

"If that's all you know about it, you may stand down," continued the King.

"I can't go no lower," said the Hatter; "I'm on the floor, as it is."

"Then you may *sit* down," the King replied.

Here the other guinea pig cheered, and was suppressed.

"Come, that finishes the guinea pigs!" thought Alice. "Now we shall get on better."

"I'd rather finish my tea," said the Hatter, with an anxious look at the Queen, who was reading the list of singers.

"You may go," said the King, and the Hatter hurriedly left the court, without even waiting to put his shoes on.

"And just take his head off outside," the Queen added to one of the officers; but the Hatter was out of sight before the officer could get to the door.

"Call the next witness!" said the King.

The next witness was the Duchess' cook. She carried the pepperbox in her hand; and Alice guessed who it was, even before she got into the court, by the way the people near the door began sneezing all at once.

"Give your evidence," said the King.

"Shan't," said the cook.

The King looked anxiously at the White Rabbit, who said in a low voice, "Your Majesty must cross-examine *this* witness."

"Well, if I must, I must," the King said with a melancholy air, and, after folding his arms and frowning at the cook till his eyes were nearly out of sight, he said in a deep voice, "What are tarts made of?"

"Pepper, mostly," said the cook.

"Treacle," said a sleepy voice behind her.

"Collar that Dormouse!" the Queen shrieked out. "Behead that Dormouse! Turn that Dormouse out of court! Suppress him! Pinch him! Off with his whiskers!"

For some minutes the whole court was in confusion, getting the Dormouse turned out, and by the time they had settled down again the cook had disappeared.

"Never mind!" said the King, with an air of great relief. "Call the next witness." And he added in an undertone to the Queen, "Really, my dear, *you* must cross-examine the next witness. It quite makes my forehead ache!"

Alice watched the White Rabbit as he fumbled over the list, feeling very curious to see what the next witness would be like. "For they haven't got much evidence *yet*," she said to herself. Imagine her surprise, when the White Rabbit read out, at the top of his shrill little voice, the name "Alice!"

Alice's Evidence

"Here!" cried Alice, quite forgetting in the flurry of the moment how large she had grown in the last few minutes, and she jumped up in such a hurry that she tipped over the jury box with the edge of her skirt, upsetting all the jurymen onto the heads of the crowd below, and there they lay sprawling about, reminding her very much of a globe of goldfish she had accidentally upset the week before.

"Oh, I *beg* your pardon!" she exclaimed in a tone of great dismay, and began picking them up again as quickly as she could, for the accident of the goldfish kept running in her head, and she had a vague sort of idea that they must be collected at once and put back into the jury box, or they would die.

"The trial cannot proceed," said the King in a very grave voice, "until all the jurymen are back in their proper places—*all*," he repeated with great emphasis, looking hard at Alice as he said so.

Alice looked at the jury box, and saw that in her haste she had put the Lizard in head downward, and the poor little thing was waving its tail about in a melancholy way, being quite unable to move. She soon got it out again, and put it right. "Not that it signifies much," she said to herself; "I should think it would be *quite* as much use in the trial one way up as the other."

As soon as the jury had a little recovered from the shock of being upset, and their slates and pencils had been found and handed back to them, they set to work very diligently to write out a history of the accident, all except the Lizard, who seemed too much overcome to do anything but sit with its mouth open, gazing up into the roof of the court.

"What do you know about this business?" the King said to Alice.

"Nothing," said Alice.

"Nothing *whatever?*" persisted the King.

"Nothing whatever," said Alice.

"That's very important," the King said, turning to the jury.

They were just beginning to write this down on their slates, when the White Rabbit interrupted.

"*Un*important, your Majesty means, of course," he said in a very respectful tone, but frowning and making faces at him as he spoke.

"*Un*important, of course, I meant," the King hastily said, and went on to himself in an undertone, "important— unimportant—unimportant—important"—as if he were trying which word sounded best.

Some of the jury wrote it down "important," and some "unimportant." Alice could see this, as she was near enough to look over their slates; "but it doesn't matter a bit," she thought to herself.

At this moment the King, who had been for some time busily writing in his notebook, called out "Silence!" and read out from his book, "Rule Forty-two. *All persons more than a mile high to leave the court.*"

Everybody looked at Alice.

"*I'm* not a mile high," said Alice.

"Nearly two miles high," added the Queen.

"You are," said the King.

"Well, I shan't go, at any rate," said Alice; "besides, that's not a regular rule; you invented it just now."

"It's the oldest rule in the book," said the King.

"Then it ought to be Number One," said Alice.

The King turned pale, and shut his notebook hastily. "Consider your verdict," he said to the jury in a low, trembling voice.

"There's more evidence to come yet, please, your Majesty," said the White Rabbit, jumping up in a great hurry; "this paper has just been picked up."

"What's in it?" said the Queen.

"I haven't opened it yet," said the White Rabbit, "but it seems to be a letter, written by the prisoner to—to somebody."

"It must have been that," said the King, "unless it was written to nobody, which isn't usual, you know."

"Whom is it directed to?" said one of the jurymen.

"It isn't directed at all," said the White Rabbit; "in fact, there's nothing written on the *outside*." He unfolded the paper as he spoke, and added, "It isn't a letter after all; it's a set of verses."

"Are they in the prisoner's handwriting?" asked another of the jurymen.

"No, they're not," said the White Rabbit, "and that's the queerest thing about it." (The jury all looked puzzled.)

"He must have imitated somebody else's hand," said the King. (The jury all brightened up again.)

"Please, your Majesty," said the Knave, "I didn't write it, and they can't prove I did; there's no name signed at the end."

"If you didn't sign it," said the King, "that only makes the matter worse. You *must* have meant some mischief, or else you'd have signed your name like an honest man."

There was a general clapping of hands at this; it was the first really clever thing the King had said that day.

"That *proves* his guilt," said the Queen.

"It proves nothing of the sort!" said Alice. "Why, you don't even know what they're about!"

"Read them," said the King.

The White Rabbit put on his spectacles. "Where shall I begin, please, your Majesty?" he asked.

"Begin at the beginning," the King said gravely, "and go on till you come to the end; then stop."

These were the verses the White Rabbit read:

"They told me you had been to her,
And mentioned me to him:
She gave me a good character,
But said I could not swim.

He sent them word I had not gone
(We know it to be true):
If she should push the matter on,
What would become of you?

I gave her one, they gave him two,
You gave us three or more;
They all returned from him to you,
Though they were mine before.

If I or she should chance to be
Involved in this affair,
He trusts to you to set them free,
Exactly as we were.

My notion was that you had been
(Before she had this fit)
An obstacle that came between
Him, and ourselves, and it.

Don't let him know she liked them best,
For this must ever be
A secret, kept from all the rest,
Between yourself and me."

"That's the most important piece of evidence we've heard yet," said the King, rubbing his hands; "so now let the jury—"

"If any one of them can explain it," said Alice (she had grown so large in the last few minutes that she wasn't a bit afraid of interrupting him), "I'll give him sixpence. *I* don't believe there's an atom of meaning in it."

The jury all wrote down on their slates, "*She* doesn't believe there's an atom of meaning in it," but none of them attempted to explain the paper.

"If there's no meaning in it," said the King, "that saves a world of trouble, you know, as we needn't try to find any. And yet I don't know," he went on, spreading out the verses on his knee, and looking at them with one eye: "I seem to see some meaning in them, after all. '—*said I could not swim*'— you can't swim, can you?" he added, turning to the Knave.

The Knave shook his head sadly. "Do I look like it?" he said. (Which he certainly did *not*, being made entirely of cardboard.)

"All right, so far," said the King, and he went on muttering over the verses to himself: "'*We know it to be true*'—that's the jury, of course—'*I gave her one, they gave him two*'—why, that must be what he did with the tarts, you know—"

"But it goes on, '*They all returned from him to you*,'" said Alice.

"Why, there they are!" said the King triumphantly, pointing to the tarts on the table. "Nothing can be clearer than *that*. Then again— '*before she had this fit*'—you never had fits, my dear, I think?" he said to the Queen.

"Never!" said the Queen furiously, throwing an inkstand at the Lizard as she spoke. (The unfortunate little Bill had left off writing on his slate with one finger, as he found it made no mark; but he now hastily began again, using the ink that was trickling down his face, as long as it lasted.)

"Then the words don't *fit* you," said the King, looking around the court with a smile. There was a dead silence.

"It's a pun!" the King added in an angry tone, and everybody laughed. "Let the jury consider their verdict," the King said, for about the twentieth time that day.

"No, no!" said the Queen. "Sentence first—verdict afterward."

"Stuff and nonsense!" said Alice loudly. "The idea of having the sentence first!"

"Hold your tongue!" said the Queen, turning purple.

"I won't!" said Alice.

"Off with her head!" the Queen shouted at the top of her voice. Nobody moved.

"Who cares for you?" said Alice (she had grown to her full size by this time). "You're nothing but a pack of cards!"

At this the whole pack rose up into the air, and came flying down upon her; she gave a little scream, half of fright and half of anger, and tried to beat them off, and found herself lying on the bank, with her head in the lap of her sister, who was gently brushing away some dead leaves that had fluttered down from the trees onto her face.

"Wake up, Alice dear!" said her sister. "Why, what a long sleep you've had!"

"Oh, I've had such a curious dream!" said Alice, and she told her sister, as well as she could remember them, all these strange Adventures of hers that you have just been reading about; and when she had finished, her sister kissed her, and said, "It *was* a curious dream, dear, certainly; but now run in to your tea; it's getting late." So Alice got up and ran off, thinking while she ran, as well she might, what a wonderful dream it had been.

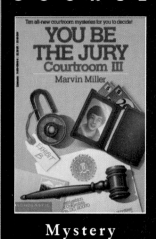
from

YOU BE THE JURY

by Marvin Miller

ORDER IN THE COURT!

LADIES AND GENTLEMEN OF THE JURY:

This court is now in session. My name is Judge John Dennenberg. You are the jury, and the trial is set to begin.

You have a serious responsibility. Will the innocent be sent to jail and the guilty go free? Let's hope not. Your job is to make sure that justice is served. Read the case carefully. Study the evidence presented and then decide.

Guilty Or Not Guilty?? →

Both sides of the case will be presented to you. The person who has the complaint is called the *plaintiff*. He or she has brought the case to court. If a crime is involved, the State is the accuser.

The person being accused is called the *defendant*. The defendant is pleading his or her innocence and presents a much different version of what happened.

In this case, three pieces of evidence will be presented as exhibits A, B, and C. Examine the exhibits very carefully. A *clue* to the solution of the case will be found there. It will directly point to the innocence or guilt of the accused.

Remember, each side will try to convince you that his or her version is what actually happened. But you must make the final decision.

The Case of the Filbert Flub

LADIES AND GENTLEMEN OF THE JURY:

When a person obtains something valuable by means of trickery, it is the same as stealing.

Keep this in mind as you decide the case before you today.

Otis Oats, the plaintiff, is suing his neighbor Brad Sweeny for tricking him into giving up a rare postage stamp. Brad Sweeny, the defendant, claims that Oats is mistaken. The rare stamp had been in his collection for years.

Otis Oats has testified as follows:

"I had just returned from visiting my Aunt Emma in Urbanville. She gave me an old family chest to keep. It had lots of old letters and postcards in it.

"When I got home, I looked through the chest. The stamps on the envelopes seemed kind of unusual. I thought some might be valuable. That's when I phoned Brad. His hobby is stamp collecting. It all started when his grandmother gave him her collection years ago. I figured if anyone would know about my stamps, it would be Brad."

The two friends went through the envelopes. After examining them carefully, Brad Sweeny told Oats the stamps weren't worth any more than they had been the day they were printed.

Otis Oats continued his testimony:

"I was disappointed. I told Brad to help himself to any stamps he wanted. He took an envelope that had a stamp with a picture of Filmore Filbert, the inventor of the supernail."

Several months later, Otis Oats read in a newspaper that Sweeny had sold his entire stamp collection, including a very rare stamp worth thousands of dollars. The newspaper had a picture of this stamp.

Oats was very upset. The stamp looked exactly like the one he had given Brad Sweeny, and which Sweeny had told him was worthless.

The envelope with the stamp attached, which Oats says he gave to Sweeny, has been entered as EXHIBIT A.

The Filmore Filbert stamp is known by collectors as the "Filbert flub." When it was originally printed, the artist accidentally drew an extra finger on Filbert's left hand.

The mistake was quickly caught, the hand redrawn, and new stamps printed. But some "Filbert flubs" were already in circulation. Today the "Filbert flub" is very valuable.

A close-up of this rare stamp appears as EXHIBIT B. Filmore Filbert is pictured holding his supernail, a nail that can be hammered into anything. You will note the six fingers on Filbert's left hand.

Otis Oats explained to the court why he is certain the rare stamp is his:

"I visited Brad Sweeny's house lots of times. He was proud of his stamp collection and he always showed it to me. In fact, I got a little bored from seeing it so much. But Brad never showed me the "Filbert flub" stamp. If it were so valuable, he would have been proud to show it to me."

Otis Oats claims that Brad Sweeny took the envelope he gave him with the "Filbert flub" stamp and erased the address. Over it, Sweeny wrote the name and address of his own grandmother, Nora Sweeny. That way Sweeny could say the letter with the rare stamp was addressed to her.

Brad Sweeny says that Otis Oats is mistaken. He explained to the court how he got the rare stamp:

"That's my grandmother's name and address on the envelope. She gave it to me. Grandma was a serious stamp collector. She began collecting in 1920, when she was only ten years old. She was even written up in the newspapers."

Brad Sweeny showed as EXHIBIT C an article describing his grandmother's collection.

A crime lab expert was called in to examine the envelope with the stamp. A special method of chemical analysis was used. Because the envelope was very old, the laboratory expert was unsure whether the original name and address were erased.

Brad Sweeny continued his testimony:

"Even if there were eraser marks, it doesn't prove anything. The letter was addressed in pencil and the person sending it to my grandmother could have made a mistake in her address, erased it, and corrected the mistake."

LADIES AND GENTLEMEN OF THE JURY:

You have just heard the Case of the Filbert Flub. You must decide the merits of Otis Oats's claim. Be sure to carefully examine the evidence in EXHIBITS A, B, and C.

Was the stamp that Brad Sweeny sold from his own collection? Or was it the stamp Otis Oats gave him?

AIRVIEW, IOWA
OCT 3
1920

Mrs. Nora Sweeny
538 N. Second Street
Madison, Iowa

WATER CONSERVATION
UNITED STATES POSTAGE
4¢

2¢
USA

UNITED STATES POSTAGE
FOUNDER OF THE
AMERICAN RED CROSS
CLARA BARTON
3¢

United States Postage
3¢

LIBRARY FEATURES STAMP COLLECTION

The Madison Public Library will have an exhibit of the stamp collection of local resident Mrs. Nora Sweeny.

Her collection includes hundreds of unusual stamps, including several that are quite rare.

Mrs. Sweeny has been collecting stamps since she was a youngster.

"I got interested in stamps when I was ten years old, some thirty years ago," said Sweeny. "The library asked if they could be displayed for the townsfolk to see. I think it's a wonderful idea."

Mrs. Sweeny has shown her collection at many antiquarian exhibits in the state.

Library hours are 9 a.m. to 5 p.m. Closed on Sundays.

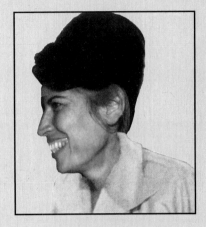

Nora Sweeny

Exhibit C

VERDICT

SWEENY TRICKED OATS INTO GIVING HIM THE STAMP.

The envelope with the Fillmore Filbert stamp in EXHIBIT A is addressed to Sweeny's grandmother, Mrs. Nora Sweeny. The date on the envelope shows it was mailed in 1920. But Sweeny testified that his grandmother began collecting stamps in 1920 when she was only ten years old.

That means Nora was ten years old when the letter was mailed. She wouldn't have been a "Mrs.," then, and she would have had her unmarried last name.

Brad Sweeny erased the name on the envelope Otis Oats gave him and substituted his grandmother's name. But he forgot she was too young to be the Mrs. Nora Sweeny.

Mary Ann Vial Lemmon

Judge

A judge *ensures* justice for all.

Judge Mary Ann Vial Lemmon knows the law—that's her job. She is a general jurisdiction judge in Hahnville, Louisiana, which means she hears all kinds of cases, from criminal cases to traffic cases. Judge Lemmon works to protect the rights of the people who come before her and of all others in her community. It's her job to apply the law fairly and impartially. It's a difficult job and a very important one. How does she do it?

PROFILE

Name:
Mary Ann Vial Lemmon

Occupation:
judge

Education:
Loyola Law School

Jobs that prepared her to become a judge:
working as a lawyer; raising six children

Community involvement:
presides over mock trials with school children

Favorite books in sixth grade:
Wuthering Heights, Oliver Twist, The Scarlet Letter, A Tale of Two Cities

UESTIONS
for Judge Lemmon

Learn *how* one judge upholds the law.

 How did you become a judge?

 Almost always, a judge starts off by becoming a lawyer. I went to Loyola Law School in New Orleans. My father went there, and three of my children have gone there, too. Another one of my children is there now, so Loyola is a real family tradition.

 What happened after you became a lawyer?

 First of all, to become a lawyer you have to pass a tough exam called a bar exam. Then you must practice law for several years before you qualify to become a judge. In some states, like Louisiana, judges are elected. In other states, they're appointed by the governor of the state.

 Can you describe a typical day?

 What a lot of people don't realize is that the majority of time that a judge spends judging is not in the courtroom. It's back in the chambers and in the books. A tremendous amount of reading is necessary to do my job effectively. I also need to think and reflect a lot to be sure that a correct decision has been reached. Whatever is decided impacts people's lives in a very serious way.

ST. CHARLES PARISH COURTHOUSE
15045

 What happens in the courtroom?

 In a case where there is no jury, the witnesses present their testimony to me. I also listen to the arguments of attorneys, who try to convince me that their side is the correct one. After hearing all the evidence that is brought before me in the courtroom, I have to decide if a law has been broken.

What steps do you take to make your decision?

It varies from case to case. We have a wonderful staff that helps to research the cases. I also have a law clerk who spends long hours researching and double-checking my own research.

What types of research do you use?

We do two things. We look at the statutes, or the laws, of the state. And we also look at cases from the past. We have centuries of other cases that guide us in our decisions. Looking at them helps us figure out how the statutes should be applied to a particular case.

As a judge, how do you act to protect a person's rights?

All people who come into court have the right to a fair trial. So by acting as a fair and impartial judge, I uphold these rights. Also, one of the instructions that a judge gives to the jury is that the defendant is innocent until proven guilty beyond a reasonable doubt. That's another right I have to uphold.

Why is our justice system so important to the community?

If everybody in the community went around doing exactly what they wanted to do, we would have total chaos. Our justice system is critical in keeping peace within a community.

Judge Lemmon's
Tips for Being a Good Judge

1 Get a broad-based education. Knowing about different subjects can help you make informed decisions.

2 Remain objective. You have to be able to see both sides of a story.

3 Be tolerant. You must be very tolerant of people's differences in order to uphold their rights.

Three Stories About Justice

illustrated by Maria Korusiewicz

*What is fair? What is right? People have asked these questions
since the beginning of time. The stories told here are about people seeking justice.
Although these stories come from three different cultures and time periods,
they show that the theme of justice is universal.*

from *The Doubleday Illustrated Children's Bible*

The WISDOM of SOLOMON

Two women came to Solomon for help one day, and with them they brought a baby boy. "My lord King," said the first woman, "this child is mine. The other woman stole him from me while I slept, because her own baby had died. Now she says this one is hers, not mine; but I am telling the truth."

And the second woman said, "You are lying! This is my child!" And the first woman cried, "That is not true! I swear that this child, who is alive, is my own!" There in the court they stood shouting and quarreling with all their might before the king; and everyone looked at Solomon to see what he would do.

"Bring me a sword," ordered King Solomon. And when the sword had been brought, he said, "There is a way to settle this. Cut the living child in two; then each of you may have half of him." When she heard this, the second woman shrugged her shoulders, but the first cried out, "No! No! Let her have him if she must, but do not hurt my son!"

And King Solomon smiled. "Put away the sword," he said. "Do not hurt the child. Now we know which one is his mother. The second woman only wanted him for her own satisfaction. But it is the true mother who will bring misery upon herself before she will allow her child to suffer harm."

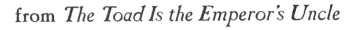

from *The Toad Is the Emperor's Uncle*

The FLY

by Mai Vo-Dinh

Everyone in the village knew the usurer, a rich and smart man. Having accumulated a fortune over the years, he settled down to a life of leisure in his big house surrounded by an immense garden and guarded by a pack of ferocious dogs. But still unsatisfied with what he had acquired, the man went on making money by lending it to people all over the county at exorbitant rates. The usurer reigned supreme in the area, for numerous were those who were in debt to him.

One day, the rich man set out for the house of one of his peasants. Despite repeated reminders, the poor laborer just could not manage to pay off his long-standing debt. Working himself to a shadow, the peasant barely succeeded in making ends meet. The moneylender was therefore determined that if he could not get his money back this time, he would proceed to confiscate some of his debtor's most valuable belongings. But the rich man found no one at the peasant's house but a small boy of eight or nine playing alone in the dirt yard.

"Child, are your parents home?" the rich man asked.

"No, sir," the boy replied, then went on playing with his sticks and stones, paying no attention whatever to the man.

"Then, where are they?" the rich man asked, somewhat irritated, but the little boy went on playing and did not answer.

When the rich man repeated his query, the boy looked up and answered, with deliberate slowness, "Well, sir, my father has gone to cut living trees and plant dead ones and my mother is at the market place selling the wind and buying the moon."

"What? What in heaven are you talking about?" the rich man commanded. "Quick, tell me where they are, or you will see what this stick can do to you!" The bamboo walking stick in the big man's hand looked indeed menacing.

After repeated questioning, however, the boy only gave the same reply. Exasperated, the rich man told him, "All right, listen to me! I came here today to take the money your parents owe me. But if you tell me where they really are and what they are doing, I will forget all about the debt. Is that clear to you?"

"Oh, sir, why are you joking with a poor little boy? Do you expect me to believe what you are saying?" For the first time the boy looked interested.

"Well, there is heaven and there is earth to witness my promise," the rich man said, pointing up to the sky and down to the ground.

But the boy only laughed. "Sir, heaven and earth cannot talk and therefore cannot testify. I want some living thing to be our witness."

Catching sight of a fly alighting on a bamboo pole nearby, and laughing inside because he was fooling the boy, the rich man proposed, "There is a fly. He can be our witness. Now, hurry and tell me what you mean when you say that your father is out cutting living trees and planting dead ones, while your mother is at the market selling the wind and buying the moon."

Looking at the fly on the pole, the boy said, "A fly is a good enough witness for me. Well, here it is, sir. My father has simply gone to cut down bamboos and make a fence with them for a man near the river. And my mother . . . oh, sir, you'll keep your promise, won't you? You will free my parents of all their debts? You really mean it?"

"Yes, yes, I do solemnly swear in front of this fly here." The rich man urged the boy to go on.

"Well, my mother, she has gone to the market to sell fans so she can buy oil for our lamps. Isn't that what you would call selling the wind to buy the moon?"

Shaking his head, the rich man had to admit inwardly that the boy was a clever one. However, he thought, the little genius still had much to learn, believing as he did that a fly could be a witness for anybody. Bidding the boy good-bye, the man told

him that he would soon return to make good his promise.

A few days had passed when the moneylender returned. This time he found the poor peasant couple at home, for it was late in the evening. A nasty scene ensued, the rich man claiming his money and the poor peasant apologizing and begging for another delay. Their argument awakened the little boy who ran to his father and told him, "Father, father, you don't have to pay your debt. This gentleman here has promised me that he would forget all about the money you owe him."

"Nonsense," the rich man shook his walking stick at both father and son. "Nonsense, are you going to stand there and listen to a child's inventions? I never spoke a word to this boy. Now, tell me, are you going to pay or are you not?"

The whole affair ended by being brought before the mandarin who governed the county. Not knowing what to believe, all the poor peasant and his wife could do was to bring their son with them when they went to court. The little boy's insistence about the rich man's promise was their only encouragement.

The mandarin began by asking the boy to relate exactly what had happened between himself and the moneylender. Happily, the boy hastened to tell about the explanations he gave the rich man in exchange for the debt.

"Well," the mandarin said to the boy, "if this man here has indeed made such a promise, we have only your word for it. How do we know that you have not invented the whole story yourself? In a case such as this, you need a witness to confirm it, and you have none." The boy remained calm and declared that naturally there was a witness to their conversation.

"Who is that, child?" the mandarin asked.

"A fly, Your Honor."

"A fly? What do you mean, a fly? Watch out, young man, fantasies are not to be tolerated in this place!" The mandarin's benevolent face suddenly became stern.

"Yes, Your Honor, a fly. A fly which was alighting on this gentleman's nose!" The boy leaped from his seat.

"Insolent boy, that's a pack of lies!" The rich man roared indignantly, his face like a ripe tomato. "The fly was *not* on my nose; *he was on the housepole . . .*" But he stopped dead. It was, however, too late.

The majestic mandarin himself could not help bursting out laughing. Then the audience burst out laughing. The boy's parents too, although timidly, laughed. And the boy, and the rich man himself, also laughed. With one hand on his stomach, the mandarin waved the other hand toward the rich man:

"Now, now, that's all settled. You have indeed made your promises, dear sir, to the child. *Housepole or no housepole, your conversation did happen after all!* The court says you must keep your promise."

And still chuckling, he dismissed all parties.

The STONE in the TEMPLE

an Islamic legend retold by Aaron Shepard

The sons of Makhzum should raise the Black Stone," declared one of the men in the circle. "It is our right as foremost of the tribes."

"Who gave you such a position?" demanded another man.

"The sons of Jumah will raise it!"

"Not while the sons of Abdu Manaf stand here," said another. "The honor should be ours."

"Then you will have to fight for it," cried another. "None but the sons of Abdul-Dar shall raise the stone!"

In the years before Muhammad's holy mission, it happened that the tribes around Mecca decided to rebuild their temple, the Kaaba. In those days, the Kaaba was only a yard enclosed by a wall. Their plan was to build a higher, thicker wall and add a roof.

Each tribe had chosen a section of the wall and started pulling down the stones. The sacred Black Stone, built into the east corner, had been removed carefully and set aside.

At last they had gotten down to the foundation laid by Abraham. They had begun to rebuild, and the wall had grown steadily higher. But when the time had come to raise the Black Stone back to its place, they could not agree on which tribe would have the honor.

The dispute grew fiercer and fiercer, till it seemed likely that blood would flow. But then Abu Amayya said, "Brothers, let us not fight among ourselves. I have an idea: Wait for the next man who comes through the gate, then give the decision to him."

All agreed and settled down to wait. And it happened that the first man to enter the gate was Muhammad, he whom they called "The Trustworthy One."

When Muhammad had listened to their claims, he considered for a moment. Then he said, "Bring me a cloak."

They brought one, and Muhammad spread it on the ground. Then he took the Black Stone and placed it in the center.

"Each tribe will choose a man to hold the cloak by its edge. Then all will raise the stone together."

This was done, and Muhammad himself set the stone in place. Then all the tribes were satisfied, and work went on with no further dispute.

How to
Write a Law

A law declares where it applies.

A law tells to whom it applies.

Each part of the law states an important detail.

In every society, people live according to certain rules, or laws. In some societies, laws are ordered by the ruler, regardless of the opinions or feelings of the people. Those governments are known as dictatorships. The United States is a democracy. In our system of government, laws are voted on.

What is a law? A law is a set of rules that the community agrees to follow. In the United States, we elect government representatives, who propose new laws. Each proposal is voted on, and if passed, it becomes law. Once a law is passed, everyone must obey it—even the people who voted against it.

CALIFORNIA VEHICLE CODE NO. 21212
OPERATION OF BICYCLES

(a) A person under 18 years of age shall not operate a bicycle, or ride upon a bicycle as a passenger, upon a street, bikeway, or any other public bicycle path or trail unless that person is wearing a properly fitted and fastened bicycle helmet that meets the standards of the American National Standards Institute. . . . This requirement also applies to a person who rides upon a bicycle while in a restraining seat that is attached to the bicycle or in a trailer towed by the bicycle.

(b) Any helmet sold or offered for sale for use by operators and passengers of bicycles shall be conspicuously labeled in accordance with the standard described in (a).

(c) No person shall sell or offer for sale for use by an operator or passenger of a bicycle any safety helmet which is not of a type meeting requirements.

(d) (1) A person who violates a requirement of this section shall be warned of the violation by the enforcing official, but shall not be issued a notice to appear.

(2) Any charge shall be dismissed when the person charged alleges in court, under oath, that the charge against the person is the first charge against that person, unless it is otherwise established in court that the charge is not the first charge against the person.

(e) (1) Except as provided in (d), a violation of this section is an infraction punishable by a fine of not more than twenty-five dollars ($25).

(2) The parent or legal guardian having control or custody of a minor whose conduct violates this section shall be jointly and severally liable with the minor for the amount of the fine imposed pursuant to this subdivision.

A law tells what will happen if it is violated.

1 Pick an Issue

Do you think that in-line skaters should be required to wear helmets and protective pads? Do you think that land should be set aside for a community garden? What changes would be helpful to your community? Write down some ideas for improvements. Then pick one issue you'd like to write a law for.

YES

NO

TOOLS

- paper and pencil

- small pieces of paper for voting ballots

- empty box or hat in which to collect ballots

2 Do Research

Once you've decided on an issue, think about why a law is needed on this subject. Will it help protect people? Will it help improve your community? Now you can begin your research. Look in newspapers and magazines to see if you can find articles about your issue. Try talking with people who may have an opinion about your issue and take a survey among them. Find out what they think about the issue. Do they think it is important? Do they agree that it will help the community?

NO

Tip Use the information from your survey to help you write the details of your proposed law.

3 Draft Your Law

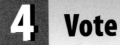

When you've gathered enough information, write your law. Start by giving your law a name, and write the place in which it will be enforced. Then write the date it will go into effect. Next, write two paragraphs describing the law. In your first paragraph, state who must obey this law, and where and when they must obey it. In your second paragraph, describe what will happen to people who disobey this law. If there is a fine as a penalty, where will the penalty money go?

4 Vote

Present your law to your class, and make sure everyone understands it. Now it's time for a vote. Ask your classmates to write "yes" on their ballots if they want the law passed, or "no" if they don't. Have the voters fold their ballots and put them into an empty box or hat. Then, count the votes. If more people wrote "yes" than "no," your law is passed!

If You Are Using a Computer ...

Use the Report format to write your law. The electronic thesaurus will help you find the exact wording you need. Create ballots with the Card format. Write the name of the law on the front of the card. On the inside, put "yes" and "no" check boxes.

THINK

What might happen if there were no laws?

Mary Ann Vial Lemmon
Judge ▶

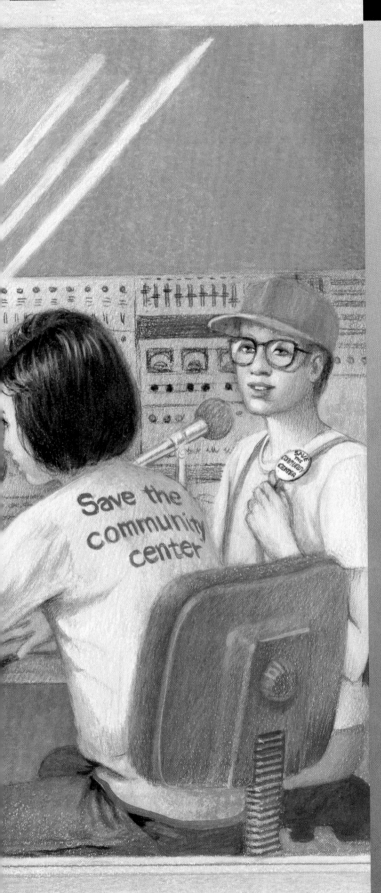

Communication advances the democratic process.

The Power of Words

Read a fable about
a man who fights
for the right to read.
Next, learn about
the first dictionary.

Discover what tools you
can use to create change
in your community. Then
see how two girls put
these tools to use.

WORKSHOP 2

Explore both sides
of an issue when
you create a point/
counterpoint chart.

Are tests a good measure of what you have learned?

POINT

Amie F. "I think tests accurately measure what I've learned. Teachers can tell what you have learned and what you haven't learned from tests. After they grade the test, teachers can go back and teach you more about what you haven't learned too well."

Jerry B. "I agree tests are good. Knowing that I am going to have a test makes me push myself more. After I study for a test, I've learned more than I knew before studying."

COUNTERPOINT

Leslie M. "I don't think tests are a good measure of what you've learned. Kids jam everything into their heads before a test so try to do well. But during the test or after the test, they forget everything they've studied."

Travis T. "Tests don't measure all the things I know. When I take a test, I feel pressured. This affects how I do. Because I get scared, I don't always remember everything I know on tests."

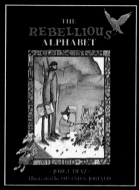
THE
REBELLIOUS
ALPHABET

By
· JORGE DIAZ ·

Illustrated by
ØIVIND S. JORFALD

The Little General was the ruler of a very big village,
even though he was very small.

He ruled the land by throwing temper tantrums and
stomping his heels on the floor.

"Rodisflankis!! Conical gransifolopods!!

"Gratz and double-gratz!! Sclonch!!"

He shouted and everybody trembled, although they didn't
understand a word he said.

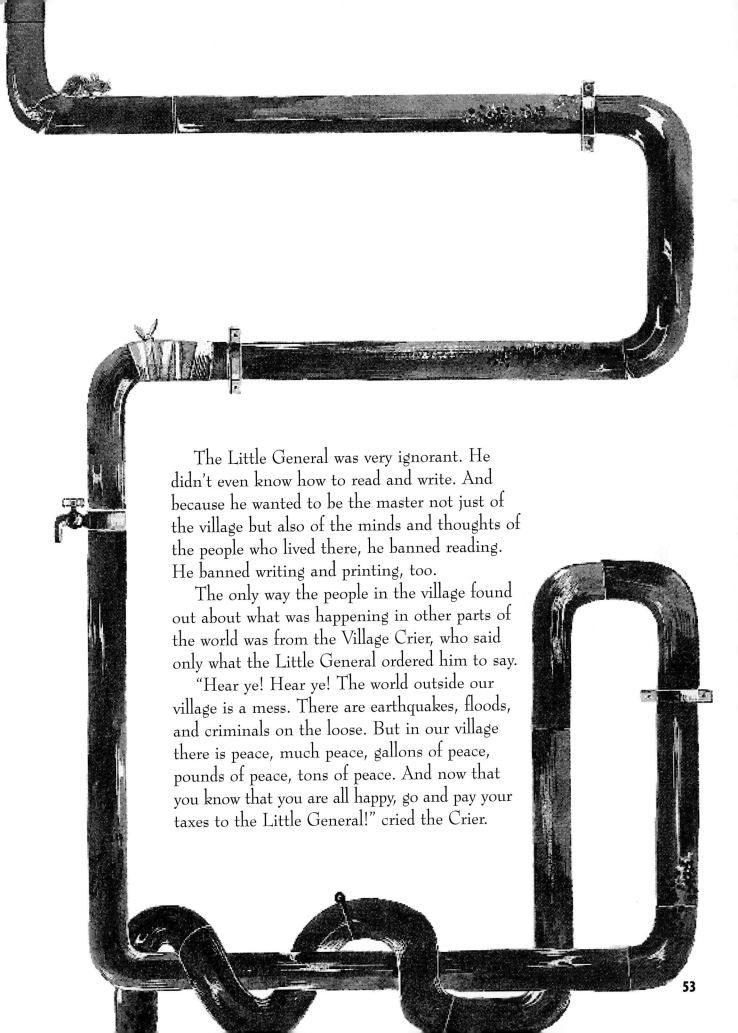

The Little General was very ignorant. He didn't even know how to read and write. And because he wanted to be the master not just of the village but also of the minds and thoughts of the people who lived there, he banned reading. He banned writing and printing, too.

The only way the people in the village found out about what was happening in other parts of the world was from the Village Crier, who said only what the Little General ordered him to say.

"Hear ye! Hear ye! The world outside our village is a mess. There are earthquakes, floods, and criminals on the loose. But in our village there is peace, much peace, gallons of peace, pounds of peace, tons of peace. And now that you know that you are all happy, go and pay your taxes to the Little General!" cried the Crier.

But there was a little old man in the village who liked to read, who liked to write, and who wanted to be the master of his own thoughts. His name was Plácido, which means peaceful.

He lived in a basement full of plants and birds, because people who are free love nature.

Since the Little General had banned reading and writing, the old man had to invent a very ingenious system to print his poems, his letters, and his leaflets. This is how he did it:

He kept seven canaries inside a large cage. Every one of them had two letters of the alphabet and one punctuation mark on each foot.

So each canary carried four letters on its stiff toes.

When Plácido wanted to print anything, he would open the cage and his canaries would perch on a sponge full of ink that he held in his hand. Then the canaries would jump up and down on a sheet of white paper, forming the words of the poem or letter or protest leaflet.

The first paper he printed was just such a leaflet—a sort of hymn to liberty—and a gust of wind carried it out through the little window of the basement where Plácido worked. It rose in the air like a comet and landed in the middle of the village square.

A farmer picked it up and read it with amazement. Awed and delighted, he showed it to his neighbors. It was the first time they had seen the word LIBERTY printed on paper!

Throughout the day the wind carried many other papers over the village. All the people living in the village talked about what was on the papers that had been printed by the little feet of Plácido's canaries. They understood, for the first time, that the Little General was tiny and ignorant.

The Little General lived in a castle, in the highest part of the village, and from there he constantly watched over each and every one of the villagers through a telescope that was three times as long as he was. Because he watched them all the time, he could see the commotion the pieces of paper were causing and the rejoicing of the people.

He ordered his men to bring some of the papers.

"Pringa rongo pluckus doublequick!! Slammettybang!! Growf!!"

His armed men ran into the village and brought him a few of the troublesome pages. When he had them in his hands, the Little General scratched his head again and again. He didn't understand a single word. He didn't know how to read, but he didn't want anybody to know that. He turned the papers around, right side up and backward, sideways and other-sideways, but he couldn't make out even a single letter.

Furious and ashamed of his own ignorance, the Little General ordered his soldiers to find the secret printing press, even if they had to look under every stone.

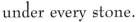

"Glup . . . scrunch shpflast!"

And they all trembled because they understood it was a
terrifying command.

The soldiers asked the villagers, but nobody told them
anything. They opened doors and climbed up to the weather
vanes and the belfries, frightening the storks . . . but they
didn't find the press.

When the soldiers were on their way back to the castle, they
saw a printed sheet of white paper whirling up in the air from a
basement window. And that was how they discovered our friend
Plácido, surrounded by papers, writing verses about liberty.

Before he was taken off to jail, Plácido asked the soldiers to
let him take his canaries with him because their songs made
him happy. The soldiers, who were really good farm boys like
Plácido himself, winked and agreed. Plácido was locked up in
a dungeon of the castle, and from there he could hear the
dreadful orders of the Little General.

"Kleenshweep brinkshpot!! Broomboom shplonket!!"

This meant that his soldiers were supposed to sweep up all
the letters they found in the village. The alphabet was to be
done away with!

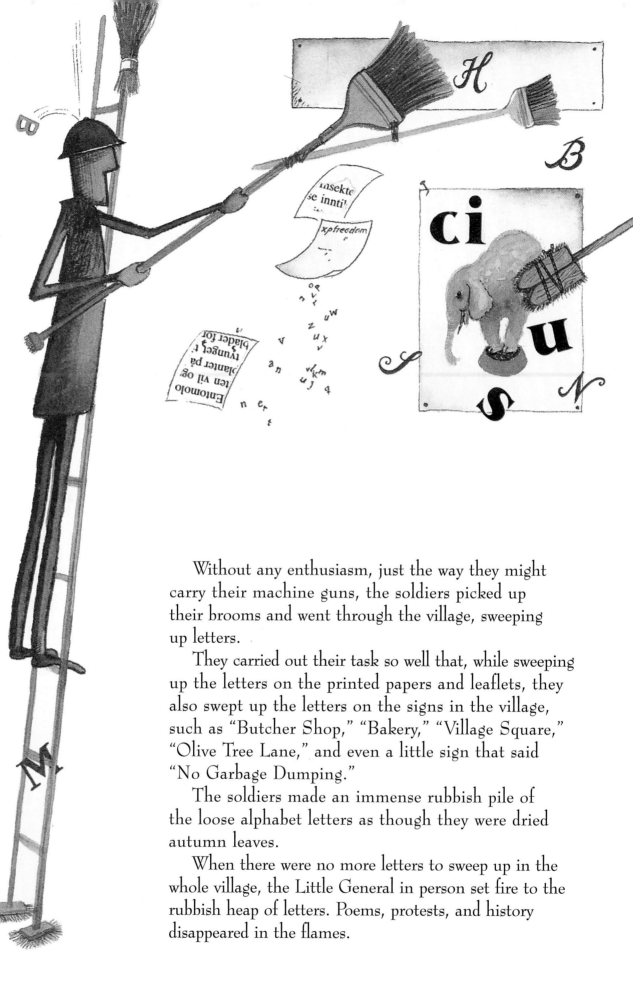

Without any enthusiasm, just the way they might carry their machine guns, the soldiers picked up their brooms and went through the village, sweeping up letters.

They carried out their task so well that, while sweeping up the letters on the printed papers and leaflets, they also swept up the letters on the signs in the village, such as "Butcher Shop," "Bakery," "Village Square," "Olive Tree Lane," and even a little sign that said "No Garbage Dumping."

The soldiers made an immense rubbish pile of the loose alphabet letters as though they were dried autumn leaves.

When there were no more letters to sweep up in the whole village, the Little General in person set fire to the rubbish heap of letters. Poems, protests, and history disappeared in the flames.

More than one villager shed a silent tear while watching the bonfire, but the tears did not put out the fire of ignorance.

The black smoke from the ink of the burned letters rose to the sky and formed a cloud that hovered precisely over the castle. The Little General thought it was nighttime and went off to bed.

"Gulp bang trinca kaput!" he said, and started to snore.

Then, unexpectedly, through the smoke and their sorrowful silence, the people began to hear the sound of Plácido's canaries.

If the canaries were singing, it meant that they had gotten out of their cage, and if they were out of the cage, it meant that they were jumping from side to side with their alphabet feet.

And in fact, even inside his cell, the little old man was printing his papers with the help of his singing, literate canaries. Their ink-spattered feet were drawing the beautiful pattern of ideas.

"Umug . . . Lopside idinumskulls!! Orolipidous remantragores!!"

The Little General had woken up and ordered his soldiers to set Plácido free because the continuous singing of the typesetting canaries kept him awake. He never did find out that the noise disturbing his sleep was really a printing shop, and that the printers worked day and night to bring words of hope to the village.

Thunder rumbled and lightning flashed, and the black cloud that had formed from the burned letters was split apart and unleashed a storm.

Black ink poured down over the castle. The Little General ran up to the tower to see what was happening. As he looked through his enormous spyglass, the ink fell on his clothes and made parallel stripes so that it looked as though he were wearing a prisoner's uniform. Seeing that, the soldiers laughed and left the castle.

It also rained on the village.

The ink fell on the walls of the houses and formed letters and words: "Liberty" . . . "Village" . . . The letters came together again on blank pieces of paper. As though they were happy little bugs, they climbed the walls and began to form names and labels: "Fresh Eggs" . . . "Shoe Repair" . . . "Dairy Products" . . .

Then the storm ended and the sun came out.

The people came out of their houses. They read Plácido's verses and understood that the Little General would never leave the castle again because he had a striped suit and was embarrassed.

And now Plácido's basement has been turned into a library, and the villagers use the Little General's telescope to look at the stars.

COMPILED BY
JAY LENO

White Flower
Two Day Sale
Friday Only

Dinosaur faces grand jury probe

Allegations of misconduct by public officials in the
energy boomtown of Dinosaur are being investigated

*The lawyer says his client
will be extinct by the time
the case comes to trial.*

Ski areas closed
due to snow

Well, let's hope it warms up soon, eh.

SOURCE

⊙CBS
RADIO
NETWORK

Radio
Commentary

NOAH WEBSTER'S DICTIONARY

from Dateline America

by Charles Kuralt

 West Hartford, Connecticut. I watched students of West Hartford's Bridlepath School compete in that vanishing standby of American education, the spelling bee. The spelling bee was held in Noah Webster's kitchen. That was a good place for it, because if it hadn't been for Noah Webster, we might never have had spelling bees or even much spelling. Before this Yankee schoolmaster came along, Americans spelled poorly or not at all; George Washington, to cite one atrocious example, spelled pretty much as he pleased. After Noah Webster, Americans spelled the way Noah told them to.

The kids in the spelling bee came from all kinds of backgrounds and from all over the country. That they speak the same language—that a kid from Maine can meet a kid from Oregon and understand him right from the start —that is Noah Webster's gift to us. His little Blue-Backed Speller sold millions of copies in his lifetime. It wore out printing presses. It was read by nearly every American who could read.

And then, working for twenty-five years, alone and by hand, Noah Webster produced his dictionary—seventy thousand words, including a lot of

American words that had never been in a dictionary before: *applesauce, bullfrog, chowder, hickory, skunk*. It was the most valuable piece of scholarship any American ever did.

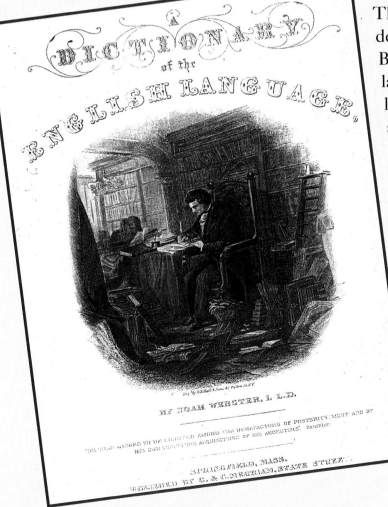 Noah Webster, from this old house in West Hartford, created American style and American manners. It is not too much to say that he created American education. He was the first teacher of American history, the first influential American newspaper editor.

"What rubbed Mr. Webster's fur the wrong way," West Hartford historian Nelson Burr told me, "was that even after the Revolution, most of America's books and most of America's ideas still came from England. He wanted to put a stop to that. He wanted to create Americanism—not in the sense of jingoistic patriotism, but in the sense of a new literature, a new language."

In the Italy of Noah Webster's day, there were so many dialects that many Italians couldn't talk to one another. The same thing, to a lesser degree, was true in Great Britain. America's common language, with more or less agreed-upon rules for spelling and punctuation, was the work of Noah Webster. He wanted us to be one nation, a new nation, and he showed us how.

Social Action Guide

FROM IT'S OUR WORLD, TOO!

TOOLS FOR CHANGE

by Phillip Hoose

▲　　●　　■　　▲

Have you ever had a great idea for solving a problem in your town? Or felt really strongly about a candidate for public office? Have you ever gotten angry about an important issue? Or had a strong opinion that you wanted to share with others? If you are like a lot of other people, you might feel there is nothing that you can do. But, in fact, there are many ways you can express your opinions, influence others and even create change. You may be surprised by the impact that you can have!

WRITE A LETTER

The price of a stamp can buy a lot of muscle. You can write a letter to request information, arrange an interview, or tell people what you think. You can ask for support, complain, try for money, or thank those who have helped you.

Here are some tips for letter writers:

▲ Put the date at the top.

■ Be personal. Say who you are and why you care.

● Get right to the point and say what you want.

▲ You don't have to type your letter, but make it neat.

■ Don't try to sound like an adult. Just be yourself.

● Address it to the right person. Often that's the local person who has the power to do what you need done. If you want to get rid of graffiti on your school, start with the school board officials rather than your U.S. senators.

▲ Use details. If you have statistics or if you can describe the problem in detail, do so.

■ Say exactly what you want the person to do.

● Keep a copy of your letter. Put it in a file and label the file so you can find it when you need it.

▲ Just close the letter with "Sincerely" and sign your name.

■ Print your name and address on the letter, so the person you are writing to can reply.

Here are some tips for pumping up your letters and turning them into "power letters":

Send copies of your letter to people your targets respect—and tell them you're doing it. Say you want to get a store to quit stocking food items that are overpackaged. If you write a letter to the manager of the store requesting the change, there's a good chance the manager will either ignore it or send back a cheerful letter that doesn't deal with your issue.

But if you send copies of your letter to the president of the company—at home—to your state representative and to the Better Business Bureau—and *say so* on your letter to the manager—he or she almost has to take you seriously. On the opposite page is an example.

Write a letter to your newspaper. Keep it brief and address it to the editor. Sign the names and ages of several in your group. The newspaper may very well print it. The letter then makes a public record of your position and gives you the chance to educate a lot of readers about the issue through just one letter.

Organize a letter-writing campaign. A national letter-writing campaign organized by Kids Against Pollution of Closter, New Jersey, caused McDonald's to switch from foam containers to paper-based wrappings. Research shows that just twenty letters to a representative about the same issue can be enough to make the issue a priority. Make sure each letter is different enough so that the representative doesn't assume they were all written by the same person.

[Date]
John F. Kennedy Middle School
Manchester, NH 03301

Ms. Loretta Lettuceleaf, Manager
Super Shop 'n' Spend
11 Monotony Drive
Manchester, NH 03301

Dear Ms. Lettuceleaf:

We are seventh-graders from the John F. Kennedy Middle School. We are writing to urge Shop 'n' Spend not to sell items that contain too much packaging.

Last Wednesday, we took a field trip to your store at the East Doldrum Mall. We counted seventy-two items that had at least four layers of packaging. We have attached a list of those products.

Some packages had hardly any food in them. Take Park Avenue cookies, for example. After you unwrap the outside plastic package, you find a cardboard box. Then there's a plastic tray with three rows inside. Each row is wrapped in plastic. There are only three cookies in each row.

What a waste! $2.59 for nine cookies and a bunch of paper and plastic. Most of this packaging winds up in our landfills, taking up space that we need. Some of it can't be recycled. We want you not to sell overpackaged products. That's the best way to send a message to manufacturers.

We want to meet with you to discuss how Shop 'n' Spend plans to solve this problem. You should know that if we're not satisfied, we plan to organize to put pressure on your store. We'll call soon for an appointment.

Sincerely,

[Names of 21 students]

cc:
Mr. Charles Chainowner, President, Super Shop 'n' Spend Co.,
7190 Comfort Court, Manchester, NH 03301
Manchester Better Business Bureau
Ms. Paula Powerbroker, Chairperson, Manchester City Council

Get to the point, and send copies to your target's bosses and others who could pressure him or her.

USE A PETITION TO BUILD SUPPORT

A petition is a statement of your position that is signed by people who agree with what you want. All those signatures make a petition harder to ignore than a letter.

A petition can:

▲ Give you a chance to educate potential supporters.

■ Give you the names and addresses of people who might stay involved in your effort.

● Give you something that will help attract the attention of decision makers and reporters.

Here are some tips for creating effective petitions:

▲ Give your petition a title that sums up the issue in a few words.

■ Make a copy and file it somewhere so you can find it easily. Don't give your only copy away.

● Make sure the petition asks the people who sign it to give their names, addresses, and telephone numbers, too. That way you know how to reach them if you need their support later.

▲ Call reporters when you deliver the petition to the decision maker.

On the opposite page is an example.

In some places, you can force a hearing or even a vote on an issue by starting a legal petition, that is, a petition among registered voters. If enough voters sign, the issue has to be discussed in an official meeting or voted on in a referendum. The rules differ from state to state and even from town to town, so you'll have to check. The secretary of state's office is a good place to start.

Even if you can't vote, it might pay to try to get voters to sign a petition. You can give copies of the petition to politicians to show your issue concerns voters, too. Most important of all, a petition gives you a chance to meet and educate potential supporters.

▲ ● ▬▬▬▬

"When you're trying to get people to sign a petition, take your time. Be patient and explain, even if you have to say the same thing over and over. The more people know, the more they will be willing to help you."

—Andrew Holleman

▬▬▬▬ ● ■

▼ **Here is a petition with a title and a brief, specific description of a problem.**

Petition for a Traffic Light at Sixth and Main Streets

We, the students of Tubman Middle School, think there should be a traffic light at the intersection of Sixth and Main streets.

It is dangerous to cross the street there. Since school began on September 6, there have been two accidents there that have injured students. There have been several other near-misses.

In the winter it is already dark by the time we get to that crossing after school. There is a lot of traffic at those hours, too, because some people are driving home from work.

Often you have to try to run when there's not enough time. We would feel much safer if there were a light.

Name	Grade	Address	Phone

SPEAK OUT

Our democratic system of government is an engine that runs on words. It sputters on through committees and hearings, speeches and testimony. To make it run your way, you have to add your voice to the fuel.

A speech makes you organize your thoughts and refine your arguments. It gives you a chance to have your views recorded in the minutes of public meetings and to get on mailing lists so you'll know of future activities. And people who care enough to speak about an issue in public command respect. "Whenever I get up to speak," says Alex Reinert, "I remind myself that it takes a lot of courage to get up in front of a group of strangers. Everyone knows that. So just getting up is impressive."

Here are some tips for making good speeches:

▲ Start by writing an outline of what you want to say.

■ Rehearse a lot. Practice on your parents, your friends, your plants, your dog, your mirror.

● Take your outline with you and refer to it if you need to when you speak. But try not to read it. Look at the people you want to convince.

▲ Smile. Try to have fun.

■ Begin by saying who you are and why you are there. Your personal experience is important. Then get right to the point. Say what you want and why you should get it. Keep your speech short.

● Bring things like photos, posters, or charts with you that will help make your point. Show them during your speech.

▲ If you get stuck, or if you don't like how you sound, stop, take a deep breath, and start again. People will understand. Everyone gets nervous.

■ If you are speaking into a microphone, try to keep your mouth about an inch away. Speak in a loud, clear voice.

USE THE MEDIA

TV and newspaper reporters are paid to come up with stories every day, even when there's nothing happening. *They need stories.* If you lay a story in their laps, a story about a confident and determined group of young people working skillfully to make an important change, chances are good you'll see yourselves on the TV news and in the next morning's paper.

But things can go wrong. Sometimes reporters arrive too early or too late or leave at the wrong time. They quote the wrong people or take a photo that doesn't show what you want. It turns out that getting publicity is easy. The challenging part is having them write the story you want.

You'll succeed if you can give reporters an exciting story with clear news hooks and things to photograph or film. In short, give them a story that practically writes itself, a story that you yourself would like to read. Here are some tips:

Get the reporter you want. Do a little digging into each station or paper. Who covers the appropriate subject, such as schools, the environment, or peace issues? Go to the library and read some of their stories. Do you like them? If not, is there a feature or general assignment reporter whose stories you like better? Call the station or paper and ask specifically for that person. Tell your story idea briefly, emphasizing the most interesting points.

Write a press release. Use it to set up the story you want to see written. Put quotes in it, so you can state your position exactly the way you want to say it. Give it to reporters before your event, and have it ready to give them again during the event. Here's an example:

Press Release

For Immediate Release

Contact: Judy Dribble
555-4431
(after 4:00 P.M.)

Lincoln Students to Protest Sexism in Basketball Program

On December 16 at halftime of the Lincoln-Washington boys' basketball game, a group of students at Lincoln School will demonstrate to protest the inequality of the resources given to the boys' and girls' basketball programs. They will march around the court carrying signs of protest and singing a new song they have made up, "Sweet Georgie Brown."

"We have to wait until the boys are finished to practice," says Lisa VanDunk, a junior forward on the Lady Bulldogs. "Some of us who live in the country don't get home until after nine." Girls also say that unlike the girls, the boys' team gets school laundry service, cheerleaders, and bus transportation to the games. "It's just sexism," says guard Alice Press.

Girls say that they play their games after school on weeknights, when few people can attend, whereas the boys play on weekend evenings. The protest will also include boys who sympathize with the girls' complaints.

When: December 16, 1992
Where: Lincoln School Gym, 12 Maple Street, Sweetwater
(rear entrance)

At an event or a press conference, use props. Try to think like a photographer: what prop would really dramatize, in a picture, what you want to say? When, at their first press conference, kids working on the Children's Peace Statue planted marigolds in the nose cone of an old missile, photographers loved it.

Decide in advance who will speak to the press. Assign that person to stay with reporters during the event.

Give another copy of the press release to reporters at your press conference. Don't assume they kept the one you sent them. Make their job as easy as possible.

Get started on time. Reporters usually want to cover the story, get back to the office, and write it up or edit video footage. Often they work on very tight deadlines. Help them by starting right on time.

Get to know reporters. Thank them. Send them updates. Think of ways to stay in touch. That way, the next time you need help, you'll know someone to call.

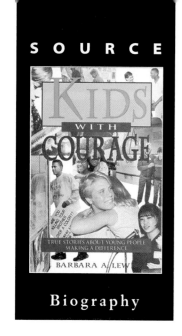

Honoring

BY Barbara A. Lewis

EDITED BY Pamela Espeland

FROM **KIDS WITH COURAGE**

THEIR Ancestors

TO RENA AND JENNA DUNCAN, THOSE

STATUES IN THE CAPITOL BUILDING WEREN'T

JUST TWO ANONYMOUS INDIANS. THEY WERE

JOHN DUNCAN AND UNCA SOM.

Rena and Jenna Duncan live about a mile apart, down dusty roads skirted with sagebrush and tall grass, nestled at the base of the Uintah Mountains in Utah. They ride horses past cedar trees and beneath low-hanging willows, over the 39 acres of pasture land surrounding Rena's white frame house. They keep all kinds of pets: dogs, cats, hamsters, whatever wanders by.

From their names, you might think they are sisters, maybe even twins. They're not. Rena is Jenna's aunt—her mother's sister—and Jenna is Rena's niece. But the two girls have grown up together like sisters. On a weekend evening, you might find them giggling together in their sleeping bags on Rena's bedroom carpet, pretending to be asleep. Rena makes up ghost stories to try to scare Jenna, who covers her head with her pillow to smother her laughter.

They're regular Native American girls. Jenna likes rap music and is a bit of a tease. She hopes to become a doctor or veterinarian someday. She's friendly and good at math.

Rena likes to draw cartoons and write stories, which she keeps locked in her secret journal. Because she is fascinated by the Anasazi Indian culture, she dreams of becoming an anthropologist.

Both girls enjoy reading mysteries. School is not hard for them. But it wasn't always that way for Rena. When Rena started kindergarten, she hated to go into the strange place where she didn't know everybody. "I'm shy until I get to know people," she admits. "Then I talk a lot."

Rena and Jenna were among the first Native American children to attend the formerly all-white Neola Elementary School. At first, school was a struggle for Rena. Instead of listening to the teacher, she would gaze out the window and imagine that she was with her father, examining an ancient Anasazi ruin.

Rena's father, Clifford Duncan, is Director of the Museum for the Ute Indian Tribe. He often shows archaeologists how to identify historical sites and remains. "I respect my dad because he knows a lot and helps me to understand the world better," Rena says.

She loves tromping along with her dad on explorations. Sometimes she stops to gather bluebells from mountain cliffs. She studies petroglyphs—drawings on cave walls—and asks, "Who drew these pictures? What were they trying to say?" Her dad weaves stories of ancient ancestors and explains what he thinks the strange little stick figures mean.

Once Rena saw a half-buried arrowhead in the dirt. As she reached down to snatch it, her father caught her by the wrist. "Rena, whenever you take something from the place that ancient people lived, you must leave something in return," he told her. "Then you are not just taking." His dark eyes held her in check, but they twinkled.

Rena pulled a red scarf from her hair and laid it on the dirt, smoothing out the corners. Her dad prayed to the ancient ones to accept the exchange. He nodded at Rena, and only then did she pick up the arrowhead.

Clifford finds other treasures in the hills. When Rena is sick, he climbs the Uintah foothills to collect sagebrush and bitter herbs for medicinal tea, which he prepares for her. Once a doctor gave her penicillin, but that made her worse. She prefers her father's tea.

Rena takes part in many Indian ceremonies performed by her father. The ancient sweat ceremonies are only for the family. Together, they sing, pray, and inhale steam from the hot rocks. In the summer, Rena watches Clifford participate in the Sundance Ceremony, fasting for three or four days and nights to cleanse his mind and body, communicating with the Creator, and renewing his attachment to the spirit of the world and nature. During that ceremony, Rena sings with the women and imagines the different roles the animals played in the creation of the world.

Sometimes Rena watches over her dad's shoulder, his black braids trailing down his back, as he paints pictures. One of her favorites shows the opening of the earth at creation, with birds flying out. She watches Clifford dip his paintbrush into somber grays, browns, and deep blue acrylics. She imagines how the world must have been at the very beginning, with all of nature singing together. She is proud that one of her father's paintings hangs in the Smithsonian Institution in Washington, D.C.

In spite of Rena's creative imagination, grade school remained a struggle for her. Nothing seemed to sink in or make sense. She didn't understand the strange symbols which stood for words. Arithmetic numbers danced around the page, refusing to stand still, as she pretended they were tiny animals.

Finally, in the fourth grade, a teacher named Mrs. Luck "turned the light on for her and brought her out," says Rena's mother, Charlene. Mrs. Luck saw strong talent in Rena. Noticing that Rena was interested in archaeology, Mrs. Luck encouraged her to enter the history fair. Suddenly school made sense to Rena. She won prizes in the fair several years in a row.

Shortly after fourth grade, Rena's dad took her to the Utah State Capitol Building in Salt Lake City. He had something important to show her. He took her to the House of Representatives and pointed to two white marble busts—statues showing the upper part of the body—at the entrance to the House chambers.

Rena saw that the busts were of Native American men. When she looked closer, she recognized one as John Duncan, her own great-great grandfather. She held her breath and looked at the other. It was Unca Som, her great-great-great grandfather! Her black eyes grew larger. She stood and stared.

Then she noticed something else—something that wasn't there. Neither statue had a name plate.

Rena calculated. For 50 years, those sculptures had watched over legislators as they bustled past, while lobbyists pressed for laws and amendments. To most people, they were just two anonymous sculptures of American Indians. But if you stopped to look at them, you could see the wrinkles at the corners of John Duncan's kind eyes, his long braids, a hint of a smile on Unca Som's face. These were stone portraits of real men.

Rena's father spoke to her of Unca Som, the medicine man. During the winter, Clifford said, "he'd chop wood in the snow for the stove. He would wear no shoes, because his belief was so strong, and the cold would not affect him."

He also spoke of John Duncan, the last great chief of the Uintah Band. As a delegate for the tribe, John Duncan had traveled to Washington, D.C., in leadership capacities. "He had many friends with Sioux, Shoshone, Navajos, and white people, too." Clifford explained. "Everyone respected the Indian leader on the great white horse. People came to trade buckskins for rugs or just to talk with John Duncan."

And then Rena's dad reminded her that she had been born in the Heber Valley. So had John Duncan. "There is a connection between you two," her mother often said.

Sometimes Rena felt that connection with the past. When she made up stories so scary that she even frightened herself, gazing about her bedroom at the black night shadows, she would suddenly feel the ancient ones watching over her. Then she would fall asleep in a sweep of peace.

Her link to John Duncan would grow even stronger. When Rena and Jenna were in sixth grade, Mr. Dallas Murray, a fifth-grade teacher at nearby Myton

grade teacher at nearby Myton Elementary, contacted the girls. He expressed concern over the fact that no names plates identified the busts of their ancestors at the Capitol building. Mr. Murray had grown up near the Ute Indian Reservation. He recognized Unca Som and John Duncan each time he took his own class to the State Legislature.

Mr. Murray suggested that they all go to the Utah Legislature to propose a resolution to put name plates on the sculptures. The girls could testify for the resolution on the floor of the House of Representatives, he explained. Rena and Jenna exchanged excited grins. They ran home and grabbed paper and pencils to begin composing their speeches.

When the day approached, Rena and Jenna fussed with their hair and chewed on their nails. They felt as if teams of horses

JOHN DUNCAN

UNCA SOM

The whole family traveled to Salt Lake City to hear the girls' speeches.

Rena and Jenna climbed the wide marble staircase to the entrance of the State Capitol. Rena felt small a she walked between tall Greek Columns and into the huge, domed lobby.

A busload of fifth graders from Myton and Neola Elementary schools had come to give their support. The thought of speaking in front of all those kids made the girls extra nervous. "I was afraid I'd mess up," Jenna remembers. Rena just waited in silence.

But as they stood to present their testimonies, the House of Representatives grew quiet. Fifth-grade children from two elementary schools sat still and listened. The legislators stopped their bustle and listened. Television and newspaper reporters listened while the high ceilings bounced back echoes of two small girls' voices.

Their voices gathered strength as they rang out their message: Respect Unca Som and John Duncan. Notice them. Respect the heritage they contributed. Don't leave their sculptures nameless.

House Concurrent Resolution 7 passed both the Utah House and Senate without one vote against it. And on January 16, 1990, Mr. Murray helped the girls to hang up the name plates. The two sculptures weren't anonymous anymore.

The following July, Rena received another surprise. She was selected to represent the State of Utah in the Native American Boy Scouts and Girl Scouts competition in Boca Raton, Florida. There she told folk tales, like "The Coyote and Its Reflection," and performed the traditional Bear Dance and War Dance. For the dances, she wore beaded moccasins, a bone necklace, and a red-and-blue native costume her mother had made from trade cloth and shells.

As Rena danced with slow, graceful movements, the bone necklace swayed. Her braids, wound in otterskin wraps, glistened. The once shy girl then answered many questions with poise and ease. She wasn't the least

RENA (SPEAKING) AND JENNA DUNCAN AT THE UTAH STATE CAPITOL.

bit afraid. After all, she had spoken before the Utah State Legislature! Rena was named a runner-up in this national competition.

When you ask her where she got her courage, Rena says, "I learned a lot about my elders as I researched and prepared my speech for the legislature. I learned to respect Unca Som and John Duncan. I felt pride inside. I felt pride and dignity to be an Indian. It was an honor to do such a thing. And now I'm not so nervous speaking before people. I'm not so afraid now."

JENNA DUNCAN'S

Testimony at the State Capitol

My name is Jenna Duncan, and I give the following as my testimony.

Unca Som was related to the Duncans on my Grandfather's Mother's side of the family, who are of the Whiteriver Band. He was an Indian medicine man who lived a very simple life. He resided on the Uintah Reservation since the Meeker Massacre, when the Whiterivers were placed there. He was believed to have been the oldest Indian that ever lived on the reservation.

He was known only as "Unca Som," which meant "Red Som." The name "Som" has no real meaning.

Little is known about Unca Som, because when you are a medicine man, you live only within the nature side of life, and the outside world has little meaning. To Indians, he was a man of the "Old Way of Life," because today we no longer have these true medicine men.

Being a descendant of this man gives me honor to give this testimony.

Thank you.

RENA DUNCAN'S

Testimony at the State Capitol

My name is Rena Duncan, and I give the following as my testimony.

My Great-Great Grandfather, John Duncan, was born in Heber Valley around the year 1857. He was born a Tumpanawach Ute, which is part of the Uintah Band as it is known today.... When the Government opened more of the Uintah Reservation to homesteading, my Great-Great Grandfather, John Duncan, was one of the delegates to travel to Washington, D.C. He also served on several other delegations to Washington, D.C. and New York on behalf of his Indian people.

Before the Indian Reorganization Act, when the Ute Indian Tribe set up their formal government system which is used today, the Utes had representatives from each band that were considered chiefs. My Great-Great Grandfather was the chief of the Uintah Band. He remained chief in 1937 although nearly blind. He died in September of 1941 and was buried in the Red Cedar Buttes in Farm Creek near Whiterocks, Utah.

My Great-Great Grandfather John Duncan was an Indian with traditional beliefs who loved his Indian people and was a friend to the non-Indian.

Even though I never knew him, he gives me pride and dignity to be an Indian, and I am honored to give this testimony on behalf of Great-Great Grandfather John Duncan.

Thank you.

How to

Make a Point/ Counterpoint Chart

The topic appears at the top of the chart.

The chart is divided in half. One side of the issue is discussed on the left. The other side of the issue is discussed on the right.

How do people prepare to debate an issue? Usually they look at both points of view, so that they can anticipate what the opposition's arguments will be. One way to see both sides of an issue is to make a point/counterpoint chart.

What is a point/counterpoint chart? A point/counterpoint chart presents two sides of an issue equally and fairly. The points from one side of the issue appear on one side of the chart. The counterpoints appear on the other side of the chart.

Are tests a good measure of what you have learned?

POINT

Amie F. "I think tests accurately measure what I've learned. Teachers can tell what you have learned and what you haven't learned from tests. After they grade the test, teachers can go back and teach you more about what you haven't learned too well."

Jerry B. "I agree tests are good. Knowing that I am going to have a test makes me push myself more. After I study for it, I've learned more than I knew before studying."

COUNTERPOINT

Leslie M. "I don't think tests are a good measure of what you've learned. Kids jam everything into their heads before a test to try to do well. But during the test or after the test, they forget everything they've studied."

Travis T. "Tests don't measure all the things I know. When I take a test, I feel pressured. This affects how I do. Because I get scared, I don't always remember everything I know on tests."

Each side has about the same amount of information.

1 Choose an Issue

With a partner, make a list of issues that people don't seem to agree on. Think about topics that people are discussing, such as saving the rain forests or reducing global warming. You might want to look in the newspaper for ideas. What are some current issues in your community? Thinking about your neighborhood or school might give you even more ideas. After writing your list, pick the issue you'd most like to discuss.

TOOLS

- paper and pencil
- newspapers and news magazines

Tip You may wish to take a survey of what community issues people think are important. Then choose an issue from your survey.

2 Research Your Topic

You probably feel strongly about the issue you've chosen. But chances are you know only your side of the question. Become an expert on both sides by doing some research. Look for articles in newspapers and news magazines that present different points of view. Ask your friends, family, and teachers for their opinions. Does your issue have something to do with your school or community? Then you might want to talk to someone who works in that area and is affected by the issue. Try to get information and opinions to support each side of the argument.

3 Make Your Chart

Now that you've collected your information, you are ready to create a point/counterpoint chart that presents both sides of the issue. Here's how to organize your chart:

1. Write the issue you've chosen across the top of the chart.

2. Divide your paper in half vertically.

3. Write the heading "Point" on the left side of the chart and "Counterpoint" on the right side.

4. In each column, write about one point of view. Use the supporting details and examples you've collected.

4 Present and Debate

Think of ways to present your chart to the class. How about organizing a debate with a partner? Each of you could defend one side of the issue. At the end of the debate, ask your audience if they can think of any points that were not covered. You also might want to send your chart to your school newspaper or a local paper to see if they'll run it in one of their issues.

If You Are Using a Computer ...

Create your chart in a two-column format on the computer. Experiment with different fonts for the title and any subtitles.

THINK

Why do you think it's important to know both sides of an issue?

Mary Ann Vial Lemmon
Judge ▶

In a democracy, people are empowered to voice their concern for others.

Taking a Stand

Discover how an eleven-year-old boy tries to save a helpless dog. Then, read about what one girl would do if she ran the world.

Find out how Eleanor Roosevelt stood up for the rights of others. Learn how Nelson Mandela fought for the rights of his people.

PROJECT

Imagine you are debating an issue. Write a closing argument.

FROM
SHILOH

BY PHYLLIS REYNOLDS NAYLOR
ILLUSTRATED BY RONALD FINGER

When eleven-year-old Marty Preston finds a small beagle wandering in the woods, Marty takes the dog home and names him Shiloh. Then Marty finds out that the dog belongs to Judd Travers, the local bully, who has a reputation for mistreating his hunting dogs. Marty's father insists that Shiloh be returned to his rightful owner, but Marty can't bear to part with the dog. Can Marty think of a plan to save Shiloh before it's too late?

I'm back to not sleeping again. Everything I can think of to try, I've already thought on and turned down. Even thought of Dad and me driving to Middlebourne and going to the county courthouse to report a man who's mean to his dogs, thinking maybe they wouldn't let Judd have Shiloh back again. Dad says that's where we'd have to go, all right, but how am I going to prove it about Judd? Think about that, he says.

I been thinking about it. Do I really suppose they'd send an investigator all the way out from Middlebourne to see about a man said to kick his dogs? And if they did, do I think Judd's going to tell the man yes, indeed, he does kick them? Do I think the investigator's going to hide out in the bushes near Judd Travers's place for a week just to see for himself?

Tyler County hasn't hardly got the money to investigate reports of children being kicked, Dad says, much less dogs. Even if I told the animal-rights people that I found a dog with a bullet hole in its head up near Judd's house, don't prove that Judd was the one who killed it.

I go out to talk to Dad about it some more while he's chopping wood, and he just says, "Son, it's hard, I know, but sometimes you just got to do what has to be done. It's Judd's dog and there's no getting around it."

Ma tries to make me feel better. She says at least I brought some joy and kindness into the life of a dog that never had any before, and that Shiloh will never forget me. But that even makes it worse. Wish he *could* forget. Keep thinking of how Shiloh's going to look at me when we drive him over to Judd's, and my eyes fill up again. Becky, she's been crying, too. So has Dara Lynn. The one good thing about it now is that the whole family loves Shiloh and we can talk about him out loud, but there's not one thing we can do. Three more days and we have to give him up.

I walk down to Friendly on Friday to talk with David Howard. David feels almost as bad as I do. I hardly finish telling about

Shiloh and he's got tears in his eyes already. David Howard's thirty pounds heavier and bigger than me, and he still don't care who sees him cry.

"I been thinking, David," I say. "You got relatives in Ohio, don't you?"

He nods.

"You think any of them would take Shiloh? Could you call 'em up and ask could they drive down here tomorrow and take him back with them, and I'll tell Judd we let Shiloh out one day and he never come back?" More lies.

But David's shaking his head already. "It's only Uncle Clyde and Aunt Pat, and she's allergic to dogs. They had one once and had to give him up."

On the way back home, I'm thinking about someplace really good I could hide that dog. The old gristmill, maybe, up by the bridge. The door's padlocked, but it don't take much to get in, 'cause the top of the building's open where some of the roof's blown away. I bet I could hide Shiloh in there for ten years and he'd never make a sound. But what kind of life is that? Couldn't never take him anywhere except after dark. Even then, he'd be so close to Judd's place, the other dogs would probably sniff him out.

Slowly the minutes and hours of Friday tick by, then it's Saturday, and our last day with Shiloh. We give him every little treat we can think of, a wonder we don't make him sick, and after supper we sit out on the back porch like we usually do. Becky and Dara Lynn are rolling around in the grass, and Shiloh limps out there to join in the fun. I show Becky how if you lay down on your stomach with your arms up over your face, Shiloh will work to turn you over. Both girls have to try it, and Shiloh does just like I said, trying his best to get those girls up on their feet.

"If Becky ever fell in the creek, I'll bet Shiloh would pull her out," Ma says.

"If I ever saw a snake, I'll bet Shiloh would kill it for me," says Dara Lynn.

I got a sadness inside me growing so big I feel I'm about to bust. That night I sleep a little bit, wake a bit, sleep a bit, wake some more. About dawn, however, I know what I got to do.

I get up quiet as can be. Soon as Shiloh hears me, of course, he's out of his box.

"Shhh, Shiloh," I say, my finger to my lips. He watches me a moment, then crawls back in his box, good as ever.

I dress, pull on my sneakers, take me a slice of bread from the loaf on the counter and a peach off the tree in the yard. Then I take the shortcut through the east woods toward Judd Travers's.

It's the only thing left to do. I'd talked to Dad, to Ma, to David, and nobody's got any more idea what to do than they did before. What I'm fixing to do is talk to Judd Travers straight and tell him I'm not going to give Shiloh back.

Rehearsed my lines so often I can say 'em by heart. What I don't know, though, is what Judd's going to say—what he's going to do. I'll tell him he can beat me, punch me, kick me, but I'm not going to give that dog up. I'll buy Shiloh from Judd, but if he won't sell and comes to get him, I'll take Shiloh and head out in the other direction. Only way he can get his dog back is to take me to court, and then I'll tell the judge how Judd treats his animals.

Halfway through the woods, I'm thinking that what I'm about to do could get my dad in a whole lot of trouble. Around here it's serious business when you got a quarrel with your neighbor and you got to carry it as far as the law. Folks ain't that fond of Judd, and most of 'em likes my dad, but when it comes to taking a man's property, I figure they'll side with Judd. I'm not makin' life one bit

easier for my parents or Dara Lynn or Becky, but I just can't give up Shiloh without a fight.

Will he shoot me? That thought crosses my mind, too. Some kid got shot down in Mingo County once. Easy as pie for Judd Travers to put a bullet hole in my head, say he didn't see me. I got my feet pointed toward Judd Travers's place, though, and they ain't about to turn back.

Still so early in the morning the mist is rising up out of the ground, and when I come to a stretch of field, looks like the grass is steaming. Sky's light, but the sun hasn't showed itself yet. You live in hill country, it takes a while for the sun to rise. Got to scale the mountains first.

I'm practicing being quiet. What I hope is to get to Judd's house before he's wide awake, take him by surprise. He sees me coming a half mile off, without Shiloh, he's likely to figure what I got to say and have his answer ready. I want to be sitting there on his porch the moment he gets out of bed.

A rabbit goes lickety-split in front of me, then disappears. I went out hunting with Dad once, and he said that when you first scare up a rabbit, it hops a short way, then stops and looks back. That's when you got to freeze. Can't move nothing but your eyeballs, Dad says. What you have to look for is that shiny black dot—the rabbit's eye. If you look for the whole rabbit, you almost never see him because he blends into the scenery.

So I don't move a muscle and look for the shiny black dot. And there it is. I wonder what's going on inside that rabbit—if its heart's pounding fierce. No way I could tell it I wasn't going to do it harm. So I go on, back into the second stretch of woods, heading for that second field.

I'm just about to come out of the trees when I stop dead still again, for right there in the meadow is a deer, a young doe. She's munching on something, and every so often she stops, looks up, then goes on eating again.

Hardest thing in the world for me to see how anybody could shoot an animal like that. Then I think of a couple winters ago we hardly had any meat on our table, and I guess I can see how a father with three kids could shoot a deer. Hope I never have to, though. I'm just about to step out into the meadow, when *crack!*

It's the sound of a rifle. It splits the air and echoes back against the hills.

The doe takes out across the meadow, heading for the woods. Its front legs rear up, then its back legs as it leaps, its tail a flash of white.

Crack!

The rifle sounds again, and this time the deer goes down.

I can't move. One part of me wants to go to the deer, the other part knows that somebody's out here with a rifle shooting deer out of season. And before I can decide whether to go on or turn back, out of the woods on the other side steps Judd Travers, rifle in hand.

He's wearing this army camouflage shirt, a brown cap, and the weirdest grin that could fit on a human face.

"Whooeee!" he says, holding the rifle up with one hand as he plows through the weeds. "I got 'er! Whooeee!"

I know he wasn't out shooting rabbits and happened to get a doe instead, because he doesn't have his hounds with him; Judd Travers had gone out that morning with the clear intention of getting himself a deer. I also know that if the game warden finds out about it, Judd's in big trouble, 'cause the deer he shot out of season wasn't even a buck.

He slogs over through waist-high weeds to where the doe lays. Bending over, he looks at her, walks around her a little piece, then says "Whooeee!" again, soft-like.

That's when I come out of the woods. He's got his back to me now, his hands on the doe's front legs, trying to see can he pull her himself. Drags her a little way and stops. And when he looks up again, I'm right beside him.

He whirls around. "Where'd you come from?" he says.

"Was on my way over to see you," I tell him, and for the first time, standing next to Judd Travers, I feel taller than I really am.

He looks at me a moment like he don't know if he's glad I'm there or not. Then I guess he figures me being there, only a kid, don't matter. "Look what I got!" he says. "Found her eatin' at my garden this morning, and I chased her over here."

"That's a lie," I say. "I was back in the woods watching her eat. She was comin' down from the hills the other way. You went out deer huntin' for anything you could get."

"Well, supposing I did!" says Judd Travers, and he hates me worse'n snot.

"Deer ain't in season, that's what," I answer. "There's a two-hundred-dollar fine for killing a doe."

Judd Travers is staring at me like he's about to crack me across the mouth. Way we're raised around here, children don't talk back to grown folks. Don't hardly talk much at all, in fact. Learn to listen, keep your mouth shut, let the grown folks do the talking. And here I am, shooting off my mouth at five-thirty in the morning to a man holding a rifle. Am I crazy or what?

"Not unless the game warden finds out, there's not," Judd says. "And who's going to tell him? You?"

All at once I realize I got Judd Travers right where I want him. One way you look at it, it's my duty to report a killed doe. The way folks up here look at it, though, that's snitching. And if I *might* could tell, but bargain not to, it's something else again: It's blackmail. But, like I said, I'd got to the place I'd do most anything to save Shiloh.

"Yeah," I say, my heart pounding like crazy. "I'll tell. There's a free number to call." There is, too. It's on Dad's hunting regulation papers. Boy, I sure didn't know I was going to step into all this when I come up here this morning.

Now Judd's looking at me good, eyes narrowed down to little slits. "Your pa put you up to this?"

"No. This is me talking."

"Well, ain't you something now! And who's to believe you?"

"I'll get the game warden up here, show him the spot the doe was hit, the blood, and when he finds the deer at your place, he'll believe me." The words are coming out quicker than I can think, almost.

"I'll tell him he was eatin' my garden."

"And I'll say different. The new game warden won't make any allowance even if the deer *was* eating your garden. You just don't shoot deer out of season no way. 'Specially a doe."

Now Judd's really angry, and his words come at me like bees. "What you trying to do, boy? Start up trouble? You think I can't put you in your place mighty quick?"

"So what you going to do?" I ask. "Shoot me?"

Travers is so surprised his jaw drops. But I'm cooking now. Nothing can stop me. Braver than I ever been in my life.

"Going to shoot me like that dog I found up here six months back with a bullet in his head?"

Travers stares some more.

"I know whose bullet that was, Judd, and I told Dad, and if folks find me up here with a bullet in me, Dad'll know whose bullet that is, too."

I can't hardly believe the words that's coming out of my mouth. Been scared most my life of Judd Travers, and here I am, half his size, talking like a grown person. It's because I know Shiloh's still got a chance.

"So what you waiting for?" Judd says finally. "Go get the game warden." And when I don't move, he says, "Come off it, Marty. Here. You take one of those legs, I'll take another, we'll drag it to my place, and I'll give you half the meat. And don't tell me your ma won't be glad to get it."

"I don't want the meat. I want Shiloh."

Now Judd's really surprised and whistles through his teeth. "Boy, you just come up here to set me up, didn't you?"

"Didn't have an idea in this world you was out with your rifle," I tell him, and that's one of the first truths I told in two weeks. "I come up here because it's Sunday, the day you said to bring your dog back, and I wanted you to know you got to fight me first to get him. Now I'm telling you I mean to keep him, and you expect to keep that deer without a fine, you'll make the trade."

"Whoa!" says Travers. "That's no kind of trade at all! If I *hadn't* got me a deer this morning, what would you have bargained with then?"

I didn't have an answer to that because I hadn't been thinking about a deal. Judd had already said he wouldn't sell Shiloh.

Judd's eyes narrow down even more till it almost looks like he's asleep. "I just bet you *would* tell the game warden, too."

"I would."

"And you're sayin' if I let you keep my huntin' dog, you're going to keep this deer a secret?"

I begin to see now I'm no better than Judd Travers—willing to look the other way to get something I want. But the something is Shiloh.

"Yes, I will," I tell him, not feeling all that great about it.

"Well, you got to do more than that, boy, because I paid thirty-five dollars for that dog, and I want forty to let him go."

For the first time, I see a thin ray of hope that maybe he'll let me buy Shiloh. "I'll get you the money somehow, by and by," I promise.

"I don't want the money by and by. I want it now. And you haven't got it now, you work for me and pay it off."

You make a deal with Judd Travers and you're only eleven years old, you take what you can get. But all I'm thinking is *dog*.

"You got a bargain," I tell Judd, and now my feet want to dance, my face wants to smile, but I don't dare let the delight show through.

IF I WERE IN CHARGE OF THE WORLD

by Judith Viorst

AWARD WINNING

Poet

If I were in charge of the world
I'd cancel oatmeal,
Monday mornings,
Allergy shots, and also
Sara Steinberg.

If I were in charge of the world
There'd be brighter night lights,
Healthier hamsters, and
Basketball baskets forty-eight inches lower.

If I were in charge of the world
You wouldn't have lonely.
You wouldn't have clean.
You wouldn't have bedtimes.
Or "Don't punch your sister."
You wouldn't even have sisters.

If I were in charge of the world
A chocolate sundae with whipped cream and nuts
    would be a vegetable.
All 007 movies would be G.
And a person who sometimes forgot to brush,
And sometimes forgot to flush,
Would still be allowed to be
In charge of the world.

From

ELEANOR ROOSEVELT

A Life of Discovery

by RUSSELL FREEDMAN

Eleanor Roosevelt, the most influential woman of her time.

First Lady

Eleanor Roosevelt never wanted to be a president's wife. When her husband Franklin won his campaign for the presidency in 1932, she felt deeply troubled. She dreaded the prospect of living in the White House.

Proud of her accomplishments as a teacher, a writer, and a political power in her own right, she feared that she would have to give up her hard-won independence in Washington. As First Lady, she would have no life of her own. Like other presidential wives before her, she would be assigned the traditional role of official White House hostess, with little to do but greet guests at receptions and preside over formal state dinners.

"From the personal standpoint, I did not want my husband to be president," she later confessed. "It was pure selfishness on my part, and I never mentioned my feelings on the subject to him."

Mrs. Roosevelt did her duty. During her years in the White House, the executive mansion bustled with visitors at teas, receptions, and dinners. At the same time, however, she cast her fears aside and seized the opportunity to transform the role of America's First Lady. Encouraged by her friends, she became the first wife of a president to have a public life and career.

Americans had never seen a First Lady like her. She was the first to open the White House door to reporters and hold on-the-record press conferences, the first to drive her own car, to travel by plane, and to make many official trips by herself. "My missus goes where she wants to!" the president boasted.

She was the first president's wife to earn her own money by writing, lecturing, and broadcasting. Her earnings usually topped the president's salary. She gave most of the money to charity.

When she insisted on her right to take drives by herself, without a chauffeur or a police escort, the Secret Service, worried about her safety, gave her a pistol and begged her to carry it with her. "I [took] it and learned how to use it," she told readers of her popular newspaper column. "I do not mean by this that I am an expert shot. I only wish I were.... My opportunities for shooting have been far and few between, but if the necessity arose, I do know how to use a pistol."

She had come a long way since her days as an obedient society matron, and, before then, a timid child who was "always afraid of something." By her own account, she had been an "ugly duckling" whose mother told her, "You have no looks, so see to it that you have manners." Before she was ten, both of her unhappy parents were dead. She grew up in a time and place where a woman's life was ruled by her husband's interests and needs, and dominated by the domestic duties of a wife and mother. "It was not until I reached middle age," she wrote, "that I had the courage to develop interests of my own, outside of my duties to my family."

"I was tall, very thin, and very shy."

Eleanor Roosevelt lived in the White House during the Great Depression and the Second World War. In her endless travels through America, she served as a fact-finder and trouble-shooter for her husband and an impassioned publicist for her own views about social justice and world peace. She wanted people to feel that their government cared about them. After Franklin Roosevelt's death, she became a major force at the United Nations, where her efforts on behalf of human rights earned her the title, First Lady of the World.

On Her Own

"Life has got to be lived—that's all there is to it."

"The story is over," Eleanor Roosevelt told a reporter shortly after her husband's death. With FDR gone, she doubted that she could play much of a role in the postwar world.

It was hard to accept Franklin's absence after a forty-year marriage. Writing to Joseph Lash she said, "I want to cling to those I love because I find that mentally I counted so much on Franklin I feel a bit bereft."

She was sixty years old and on her own. As she came to terms with her loss, she realized that the world was watching. The story was far from over. "I did not want to cease trying to be useful in some way," she wrote. "I did not want to feel old. . . ."

The new president came to Eleanor Roosevelt for advice. Harry Truman valued her insider's knowledge of Washington and was mindful of her influence. He wanted her on his side as he tried to fill FDR's gigantic shoes.

When Japan surrendered on August 14, 1945, ending World War II, Truman personally called Mrs. Roosevelt in Hyde Park to give her the news. Later he asked her to serve as one of five American delegates to the first meeting of the United Nations General Assembly, to be held in London that winter. Eleanor hesitated. She told the president that she had no real experience in foreign affairs and knew little about parliamentary procedure. But her friends urged her to accept, and finally she did, beginning "one of the most wonderful and worthwhile experiences in my life." She believed that the United Nations was FDR's most important legacy. Her appointment as a delegate was a tribute to him, she said.

The other American delegates were men: Secretary of State James F. Byrnes; Senator Tom Connally of Texas; Senator Arthur H. Vandenberg of Michigan; and Edward R. Stettinius, Jr., who was the United States representative on the United Nations Security Council. They were not especially happy with their female colleague, dismissing her as an emotional, rattlebrained woman. Without her knowledge, these four gentlemen met and assigned Mrs. Roosevelt to Committee Three, which would deal with humanitarian, educational, and cultural questions. She imagined them saying, "Ah, here's the safe spot for her— Committee Three. She can't do much harm there!" She assumed that they wanted to keep her away from committees dealing with political and economic matters simply because she was a woman. "I kept my thoughts to myself and humbly agreed to serve where I was asked to serve," she wrote.

When the London session got under way, Eleanor Roosevelt quickly became known as the hardest-working and best-informed member of the American delegation. Nothing could make her miss a meeting. When King George and Queen Elizabeth invited her to Buckingham Palace for lunch, she accepted gracefully. But she told them that she would have to leave early to attend a subcommittee meeting.

With the U.S. delegation at a meeting of the UN General Assembly, September 1947.

To everyone's surprise, Committee Three, Mrs. Roosevelt's "safe spot," turned out to be a hotbed of controversy. The end of the war in Europe had left more than a million refugees stranded in displaced persons' camps. The Soviet Union insisted on forced repatriation—all displaced persons must be returned to their homelands. Yet many of the refugees from eastern Europe were opponents of the Communist regimes that were seizing power in their countries. They feared that forced repatriation would mean imprisonment or death. The United States and other Western nations supported the right of political asylum—allowing refugees to choose their homes. The issue of refugee repatriation landed in the lap of Committee Three.

Since that was Mrs. Roosevelt's committee, it was up to her to speak for the United States. Her opponent in the General Assembly debate would be Andrei Vishinsky, the head of the Soviet delegation, one of Russia's great legal minds, and a powerful orator. "I was badly frightened," Eleanor recalled. "I trembled at the thought of speaking against the famous Mr. Vishinsky."

As she had done so many times before at lectures and press conferences, Mrs. Roosevelt spoke without notes when she addressed the delegates of the UN's original fifty-one member nations. Afterward Andrei Vishinsky delivered a fiery speech that lasted late into the night. Finally the General Assembly voted against forced repatriation. The refugees were free to choose their own homes.

The vote was a political triumph for the United States and a personal victory for Eleanor Roosevelt. The tall lady in the flowered hat had emerged as the world's foremost spokesperson for human rights. Her fellow American delegates, who had opposed her appointment, now had to eat their words.

As Senator Vandenberg put it: "I want to say that I take back everything I ever said about her, and believe me it's been plenty."

Mrs. Roosevelt had helped determine the fate of thousands of displaced persons, yet she had never seen a refugee camp. When her fellow delegates returned home at the end of the UN session, she flew to Germany on an Air Force plane and visited several camps. One of them was Zilcheim, where Jewish survivors of Nazi death camps had built a stone monument inscribed "To the Memory of All Jews Who Died in Germany."

Lending a sympathetic ear to a refugee woman in Germany.

"I am interested in every child who needs help, and I am ready to help him."

As she toured the camp, a ragged boy about twelve years old approached with his little brother, who was about six. He did not know his own name, where his home was, or what had happened to his parents. He wanted to sing for her, he said, so Eleanor and her guides stopped to listen. Standing in the mud, gripping his brother's hand, the youngster lifted his head and sang "A Song of Freedom."

Mrs. Roosevelt served as a UN delegate throughout Truman's two terms as president. During those years of Cold War suspicion and hostility, she held firm to her belief that a strong United Nations was the best hope for a lasting peace.

In 1946, she was elected chair of the United Nations' eighteen-member Human Rights Commission, which had been instructed to draft an international bill of rights. The commission's task was to define the basic rights of people all over the world, such as the right to free speech and a fair trial, or the right to an education and a decent standard of living. During the next two years Mrs. Roosevelt proved herself a skillful diplomat as she mediated among the clashing views of delegates from different nations and cultures, each with its own ideas about the meaning of "human rights."

When the commission fell behind in its work, she drove her colleagues mercilessly, insisting on fourteen- and sixteen-hour days. The delegate from Panama begged Mrs. Roosevelt to remember that UN delegates have human rights, too. She replied that their sessions would be shorter if their speeches weren't so long-winded.

On December 10, 1948, at three A.M., the Universal Declaration of Human Rights finally came to a vote and was overwhelmingly approved by the United Nations General Assembly. Then something happened that never happened at the UN before or since. The delegates rose to give a standing ovation to a single delegate—a moving tribute to Eleanor Roosevelt's leadership.

Expressed as Mrs. Roosevelt wanted, in simple and eloquent prose, the Universal Declaration has now been published in the native languages of all countries. To this day, it stands as the most widely recognized statement of the rights to which every person on this planet is entitled.

Her crowning achievement at the United Nations. She called the Declaration a "magna carta for mankind."

THE UNIVERSAL DECLARATION OF HUMAN RIGHTS

In 1948, the United Nations adopted the Universal Declaration of Human Rights. During World War II (1939–1945), millions of innocent people had been murdered because of their religion or ethnic background.

The United Nations wanted to make sure that this would never happen again. The declaration contains 30 articles spelling out people's basic rights and responsibilities.

HERE ARE SOME OF THE MAIN IDEAS IN THE DECLARATION.

All people are born free and equal. Each person has the right to live, be free, and be safe. No one shall be kept as a slave, tortured, or treated cruelly.

A person's rights should not be limited because of race, sex, language, religion, or position in life.

Each person must be treated equally under the law. No one can be arrested without good reason. Any person accused of a crime has the right to a fair and public trial.

Everyone has the right to privacy in home, family, and mail. Everyone has the right to own property that cannot be taken away.

People have the right to travel freely. They should be free to live wherever they want in their own country and to leave and return to that country.

Everyone has the right to think, believe, and worship however he or she chooses. That includes the right to express those beliefs to others.

People have the right to take part in their countries' governments in free and fair elections.

People have the right to work and to choose the type of work they want. They should have safe working conditions, leisure time, and a limit to the number of working hours in a day.

Everyone has the right to an education, which should be free and required of all in the early years.

People have duties and responsibilities to their communities. There must be laws and limits to protect everyone's rights.

SOURCE

FACES

Magazine

by Carol Gelber

When his first son was born in 1918, Henry Mandela, a chief of the Tembu people of South Africa, gave his child two names. One name, Nelson, was English. The other, Rolihlahla, was African. In Xhosa, the language of the Tembu, Rolihlahla means "stirring up trouble." It would prove to be a suitable name. Henry's son would one day lead black South Africans in their fight for justice and human rights.

NELSON
Champion of Freedom
MANDELA

Nelson Rolihlahla Mandela grew up on his family's farm in the grassy hills of the Transkei reserve, the home of the Tembu people. He spent his days herding his family's sheep and cattle or plowing their fields. In the evenings, Nelson loved to sit near the bonfire that burned outside his family's whitewashed huts. Here he could listen to the old people tell stories about a time when "our people lived peacefully under the democratic rule of their kings and their councilors and moved freely . . . up and down the country."

Nelson Mandela photographed at the age of 17.

Those days were only a memory. Before Nelson was born, white Europeans had conquered the land. Now black Africans could not vote or choose where they lived. Men had to carry a pass. They were forbidden to enter a city unless their pass showed that they had a job there. Many men had to work far from their home and could see their wife and children only once a year.

Nelson's parents sent him to a local school run by white missionaries. Although some of the students made fun of his shabby clothes, he loved his studies and was a hardworking student. Then, when he was 12 years old, his father fell ill. Nelson was moved to the home of a relative, the paramount chief, where he lived with other boys from the Tembu royal family.

In his new home, Nelson could attend the traditional African courts in which the tribal elders served as judges. He was fascinated by the elders' skill in questioning witnesses. As he listened, he developed a love and respect for law.

At age 18, Nelson enrolled at Fort Hare College in South Africa. Tall, strong, handsome, and a natural leader, he was elected to the student council. When the college took away the powers of the council, Nelson joined a student boycott. He was suspended and sent home. The paramount chief was not pleased. He wanted Nelson to give up the boycott. Nelson writes, "My guardian felt it was time for me to get married. He loved me very much and looked after me as diligently as my father had. But he was no democrat and did not think it worthwhile to consult me about a wife. He selected a girl . . . and arrangements were made for the wedding."

Nelson ran away to Johannesburg, South Africa's largest city. For the first time, he saw how Africans lived in the shantytowns outside the cities. Thousands of people lived in shacks made of cardboard and packing crates without electricity or running water. Men worked long hours for so little pay that they could not feed their families.

Nelson Mandela attends a rally for human rights.

Nelson's days in Johannesburg were long and tiring. He worked while he finished his college education by correspondence course. When he got his degree, he found a job in a white law firm. The lawyers were impressed with Nelson and sponsored his admission to law school. Every day he took the long train ride from the law office to the university. He had to return home before the curfew that applied only to black people.

In the black township where he lived, Nelson Mandela's friends were members of the African National Congress (ANC). This organization was founded in 1912 by four black lawyers to fight injustice and discrimination. The ANC wanted all the peoples of South Africa to unite in the battle for democracy. Some groups, such as the Zulu and the Xhosa peoples, had been rivals long before the arrival of the Europeans.

With Oliver Tambo, a friend from Fort Hare College, Mandela joined the ANC. Tambo and Mandela, both lawyers, opened an office in Johannesburg—the only black law firm in the city. Both men were dedicated to the fight for human rights, and they would soon be recognized as leaders of the ANC.

(above) Oliver Tambo, Nelson Mandela's long-time friend and fellow freedom fighter, was the leader of the African National Congress (ANC) outside of South Africa from 1960 to 1990.

(opposite page) Nelson Mandela spreading his message against apartheid.

In 1948, the South African government set up a system of apartheid
aimed at the complete separation of
the races. The people of South Africa
were classified into four categories:
Europeans, Asians, Coloreds, and
Bantus (Africans). Each group was to
live in areas assigned by the government. Many families were separated—
husbands from their wives and children from their parents. The mission
schools, like the one Nelson Mandela
had attended as a boy, were closed.
Black children were told to attend
Bantu schools, which would prepare
them to be farmers or servants.

Mandela and Tambo organized
an ANC campaign urging people to
refuse to accept the segregation
laws. They led boycotts, workers'
strikes, and protest marches that
made the whole world aware of the
injustice of apartheid.

In 1955, the ANC and other
groups drew up the Freedom Charter,
which stated, "We the people of
South Africa declare that South Africa
belongs to all who live in it, black and
white, and that no government can
justly claim authority unless it is
based on the will of all the people."
Mandela was arrested.

(above) Nelson Mandela speaking at an ANC conference in Durban.

(right, top) Nelson Mandela is welcomed to Zimbabwe by Prime Minister Robert Mugabe.

(right, bottom) Nelson Mandela celebrates his 77th birthday.

For the next 35 years, Mandela and Tambo spent much of their time in exile or in prison. Mandela could see his wife, Winnie, only a few times each year. Their two daughters grew up without their father. In fact, Nelson Mandela was in prison for 28 years. He became the most famous prisoner in the world.

In the mid-1980s, South Africa's president said he would free Mandela if he would renounce the policies of the ANC. Mandela refused, saying, "Let him free all who have been imprisoned, banished or exiled for their opposition to apartheid. . . . What freedom am I being offered when I may be arrested on a pass offense? What freedom am I being offered to live my life as a family with my dear wife who remains in banishment? What freedom am I being offered when I must ask for permission to live in an urban area? What freedom am I being offered when I need a stamp in my pass to seek work?"

In 1990, Nelson Mandela was unconditionally released from prison. Since then he has toured the world, speaking out for human rights. Rolihlahla still fights for justice and equality for black South Africans. And he has come to symbolize the struggle for democracy for all peoples.

> *In May 1993, Nelson Mandela became the first black president of South Africa. This election was the first time he was allowed the right to vote. In December 1993, he was named one of the winners of the Nobel Peace Prize.*

SOUTH AFRICA *at a Glance*

DATABANK

Area:	471,440 sq. mi.
Date of Independence:	1910
Total population (1995):	41,240,000
Languages:	Afrikaans, English (both official); Zulu, Xhosa, Sotho,Tswana, Venda
Capitals:	Pretoria (administrative), Cape Town (legislative), and Bloemfontein (judicial)
Largest cities (population):	Cape Town (1.9 million), Johannesburg (1.7 million)
Percent of population under age 15:	39%

Sources: The World Factbook 1994, Central Statistical Service, 1995, The Universal Almanac, South African Quarterly Report March 1995.

ECONOMY

Gross domestic product (GDP):	$108 billion (1994)
Agriculture:	4.7% of GDP Leading products: Corn, wool, dairy
Mining:	8.7% of GDP Leading products: Gold (world's largest producer), silver, platinum, coal
Manufacturing:	23.5% of GDP
Exports:	$25 billion (1995) Leading exports: Gold, platinum metals, diamonds, coal
Imports:	$21 billion (1995) Leading imports: Machinery, mining equipment, transportation equipment, computers, aircraft parts

Sources: Countries of the World and Their Leaders Yearbook 1994, South African Quarterly Report March 1995.

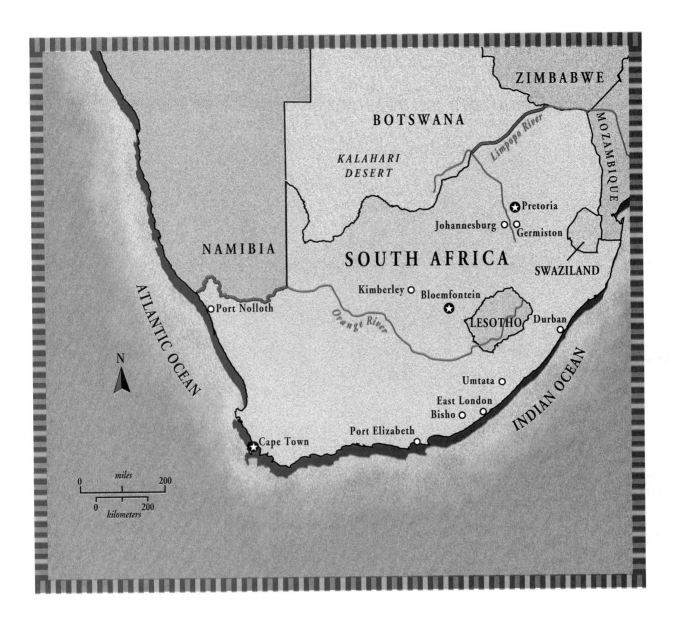

MAP

South Africa contains within its borders the independent kingdom of Lesotho, and nearly surrounds the nation of Swaziland. Apartheid, which confined black South Africans to live in 10 "homelands" (not shown here), was abolished after the April 1994 elections.

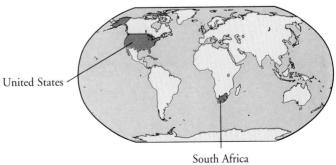

United States

South Africa

How to

Present a Closing Argument

Persuade others to agree with your viewpoint.

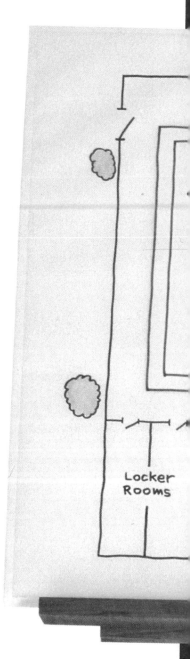

Locker Rooms

How does a lawyer influence a jury? The facts and evidence that the lawyer presents during a trial have to be very convincing. At the end of the trial, the lawyer makes a closing argument. This is the lawyer's final chance to persuade the jury—and to win the case.

A closing argument can be useful in other situations, too. In a debate, a strong closing argument can sway the judges and win the debate.

Pick an Issue

Think of an issue that's important, one that you are willing to take a stand on. It could be something that concerns your city or town, such as whether or not to build a public swimming pool and recreation center. Or there might be a school issue that you feel strongly about, such as a proposal to make the school year 12 months long. Reading your local newspaper may alert you to topics that you were not aware of before. Make a list of topics that interest you. Then choose one that you feel so strongly about that you want to persuade others to think as you do.

TOOLS

- paper and pencil

- newspapers and magazines

- tape recorder (optional)

2 Research Your Argument

Having an opinion about the topic you've chosen is not enough to win others over to your side. Just as a lawyer does, you must have evidence to support your point of view. Here are some suggestions that will help you present a convincing argument.

- **Facts:** Research facts that back up your argument. If your issue is a current one, you will find information in newspapers and news magazines. Library books will also be good sources.

- **Anecdotes:** Use brief stories that illustrate a fact or situation to make your case more persuasive.

- **Expert opinions:** Interview people who are experts on your issue. Statements by experts are especially convincing.

Be sure to keep organized notes. They will be useful when you write your argument.

How Am I Doing?

Before you write your argument, take a few minutes to ask yourself these questions:

- Did I decide which side of the issue I support?

- Did I gather enough facts and examples to support my opinion?

- Have I organized my information in a way that will appeal to my audience?

Write Your Closing Argument

To be convincing, your closing argument needs to be well organized. It should have an introduction, a body, and a conclusion.

- The introduction should grab your audience's attention. You may wish to begin with a question or a brief story that will capture everyone's interest. Your introduction will also make clear which side of the issue you support.

- In the body of your closing argument, you will defend your point of view. This is where you will present the research you did. A good technique is to include a statement of the opposing viewpoint—and then show why it isn't valid.

- The conclusion of your closing argument should briefly tie together all your points and restate your opinion. Thank your listeners for their attention. Also, express the hope that they are convinced that your point of view is the correct one.

Tip Count the number of facts in your argument. If you have one or two to support your argument, you may want to add more. It 's hard to argue against facts!

4 Present Your Closing Argument

Read over your closing argument and underline key words and phrases to emphasize as you speak. Then use a tape recorder to practice your speech. Keep in mind that making eye contact is important when you speak to an audience. Talking in front of a mirror can be helpful. Or practice presenting your closing argument to a friend. Have your friend keep track of the number of times you look at him or her as you speak. Once you've polished your speech, you're ready to deliver it to a larger audience.

An effective closing argument should persuade people to side with you on the issue you're presenting. To find out if your closing argument does this, take a poll before you speak. How many people agree with your point of view? How many people disagree? Poll the audience once again *after* you present your closing argument. Hopefully, you were able to swing people over to your point of view.

If You Are Using a Computer ...

Write your closing argument in the Report format on the computer. Use the bibliography maker to keep track of the magazines and newspapers you have used to find facts.

CONGRATULATIONS

Now you can add your voice to the other voices in your community.

Mary Ann Vial Lemmon
Judge ▶

Glossary

ac·cu·sa·tion
(ak′ yōō zā′ shən) *noun*
A charge of guilt or wrongdoing.

ac·cu·ser
(ə kyōōz′ ər) *noun*
A person who blames another person for wrongdoing.

a·mend·ments
(ə mend′ mənts) *noun*
Changes made to existing laws. ▲ amendment

Fact File

There are 26 **amendments** to the United States Constitution. The first ten amendments are called the Bill of Rights. They·were added in 1791. These rights include the right of people accused of a crime to a "speedy and public trial."

---

at·tor·neys
(ə tûr′ nēz) *noun*
People who are officially appointed to represent others in legal matters; lawyers.
▲ **attorney**

banned (band) *verb*
Refused to allow something. The teacher *banned* gum chewing in the classroom. ▲ **ban**

Thesaurus

banned
disallowed
forbade
prohibited

banned

---

cam·ou·flage
(kam′ ə fläzh′) *noun*
A disguise that alters or conceals the appearance. Military camouflage is a pattern of green and brown designed to blend in with natural backgrounds.

camouflage

col·league
(kol′ ēg) *noun*
A person one works with. The doctor spoke to her *colleague*, Nurse Ryan.

de·fen·dant
(di fen′ dənt) *noun*
A person who is legally charged with breaking the law. The *defendant* was accused of driving without wearing a seatbelt.

del•e•gates
(del′ i gitz) *noun*
People chosen to represent others. Juan and Nancy were their class *delegates* at the school meeting.
▲ **delegate**

dem•o•crat•ic
(dem′ ə krat′ ik) *adjective*
Describing a system of government by the people.

di•a•lects
(dī′ ə lekts′) *noun*
Varieties of a language spoken by the people of different regions.
▲ **dialect**

dip•lo•mat
(dip′ lə mat′) *noun*
A person who is skilled in managing relations between governments.

dis•crim•i•na•tion
(di skrim′ ə nā′ shən) *noun*
The act of treating someone in an unfair way because of the person's sex, race, or religion.

dis•missed
(dis mist′) *verb*
Thrown out of a court of law. The judge *dismissed* the charges against the defendant. ▲ **dismiss**

ex•hib•its
(ig zib′ its) *noun*
Materials produced in court and used as proof in a legal case. ▲ **exhibit**

ex•ile (eg′ zīl) *noun*
Forced removal from one's country or home.

Thesaurus

exile
banishment
deportation
ostracism

game war•den
(gām wôr′ dn) *noun*
A person whose job it is to safeguard wild animals in their natural habitats.

hounds (houndz) *noun*
Hunting dogs. ▲ **hound**

hound

a	add	ŏŏ	took	ə =	
ā	ace	ōō	pool	a in *above*	
â	care	u	up	e in *sicken*	
ä	palm	û	burn	i in *possible*	
e	end	yōō	fuse	o in *melon*	
ē	equal	oi	oil	u in *circus*	
i	it	ou	pout		
ī	ice	ng	ring		
o	odd	th	thin		
ō	open	th	this		
ô	order	zh	vision		

Glossary

hu•man•i•tar•i•an
(hyōō man′ i târ′ ē ən)
adjective
Concerned about the well-being of all people.

Thesaurus

humanitarian
charitable
compassionate
merciful

jurors

im•par•tial•ly
(im pär′ shə lē) *adverb*
Treating all sides fairly or equally.

im•pas•sioned
(im pash′ ənd) *adjective*
Filled with strong feeling. He made an *impassioned* speech for human rights.

in•flu•en•tial
(in flōō en′ shəl) *adjective*
Able to have an effect on someone or something.

ju•ris•dic•tion
(jōōr′ is dik′ shən) *noun*
The power to explain and apply the law. Judges are given jurisdiction to decide the outcomes of some legal cases.

ju•rors (jōōr′ ərz) *noun*
Members of a jury. A jury is a group of people chosen to listen to evidence at a law trial and come to a decision. ▲ **juror**

Fact File

The U.S. Constitution guarantees the right to a trial by jury to any person accused of a crime that is punishable by more than six months in jail. Juries are made up of six to twelve **jurors**.

jus•tice (jus′ tis) *noun*
The use of authority to uphold the law.

leaf•lets (lēf′ lits) *noun*
Folded sheets of paper with messages printed on them. Lauren gave out the *leaflets* announcing the talent show. ▲ **leaflet**

leg•is•la•ture
(lej′ is lā′ chər) *noun*
A group of people who have the power to make or pass laws for the state or country.

Word History

Legislature comes from the Latin words *lex*, meaning "law," and *lator*, meaning "proposer."

lib•er•ty (lib′ ər tē) *noun*
Freedom.

lit•er•ate
(lit′ ər it) *adjective*
Able to read and write.

Word History

Literate comes from the Latin word *littera*, which means "letter."

lob·by·ists
(lob′ ē ists) *noun*
People who try to influence the decisions made by members of government.
▲ lobbyist

plain·tiff
(plān′ tif) *noun*
A person who makes a complaint in a legal case.

press con·fer·ence
(pres′ kon′ fər əns) *noun*
A public event called by a person or group who agree to be interviewed by members of the press.

quar·rel (kwôr′ əl) *noun*
A discussion in which people can't agree.

ref·er·en·dum
(ref′ ə ren′ dəm) *noun*
A popular vote on an issue that has been proposed by lawmakers. The town held a *referendum* on the council's decision to build a new park.

reg·u·la·tion
(reg′ yə lā′ shən) *noun*
A rule or law that controls how something is made or done.

rep·re·sen·ta·tive
(rep′ ri zen′ tə tiv) *noun*
A member of the U.S. House of Representatives, or a member of a state's body of lawmakers.

res·o·lu·tion
(rez′ ə lōō′ shən) *noun*
An opinion or decision voted on by a group.

schol·ar·ship
(skol′ ər ship′) *noun*
A collection of facts, skills, and ideas.

stat·utes
(stach′ ōōts) *noun*
Rules or laws.
▲ statute

tes·ti·mo·ny
(tes′ tə mō′ nē) *noun*
A statement made by a person under oath in a court of law.

ver·dict (vûr′ dikt) *noun*
The finding or decision of a judge or jury in a legal case. The jury's *verdict* was that the defendant was not guilty.

Thesaurus
quarrel
altercation
argument
spat

Fact File

The United States is governed by Congress, a body of elected lawmakers. Congress is made up of two groups: the House of Representatives and the Senate.

a	add	o͝o	took	ə =
ā	ace	o͞o	pool	a in *above*
â	care	u	up	e in *sicken*
ä	palm	û	burn	i in *possible*
e	end	yo͞o	fuse	o in *melon*
ē	equal	oi	oil	u in *circus*
i	it	ou	pout	
ī	ice	ng	ring	
o	odd	th	thin	
ō	open	ŧh	this	
ô	order	zh	vision	

HON RICHARD GEPHARDT   HON CHARLES STENHOLM

representatives

Authors & Illustrators

Lewis Carroll *pages 10–25*
British mathematician Charles Lutwidge Dodgson wrote scholarly papers on logic under his own name, but he used the pen name Lewis Carroll when he wrote the children's books that were to make him famous. He wrote *Alice's Adventures in Wonderland* in 1865 to amuse a child he knew whose name happened to be Alice.

Jorge Diaz *pages 50–62*
The Rebellious Alphabet is a fable that could apply to many places at different times in history. However, the story has roots in the country of Chile, where this author was born. After being forced to leave Chile because of his political views, Diaz moved to Spain. He expresses his ideas and beliefs in his plays and screenplays. Before it became a book, *The Rebellious Alphabet* was a stage play.

Russell Freedman *pages 108–117*
An avid reader during his childhood in San Francisco, California, this author discovered early on that true stories were just as interesting as fiction. When he began writing in the 1960s, he specialized in nonfiction, and eventually turned to writing about history and great people of the past. Besides Eleanor Roosevelt, Russell Freedman has written biographies of Franklin Delano Roosevelt and Abraham Lincoln.

Charles Kuralt *pages 64–65*

His journalism career began with a job on the *Charlotte News*, and since then Charles Kuralt has been reporting on events and issues that reflect American culture. For many years his commentaries entertained millions. His commentaries and his books, including *On the Road With Charles Kuralt*, reflect his love of American history and geography.

Phyllis Reynolds Naylor *pages 92–105*

This author says that she likes to read about very ordinary people in extraordinary situations. She loves to read to find out how such characters solve their problems. Perhaps that is why she wrote a book about a boy like Marty Preston. In *Shiloh*, a Newbery Medal winner, Phyllis Reynolds Naylor makes Marty and his problems seem very real.

John Tenniel *pages 10–25*

This English illustrator died in 1914, but his illustrations, particularly his interpretations of Carroll's *Alice's Adventures in Wonderland* are still loved today. When Tenniel created his original illustrations there was no process to allow for the printing of colored illustrations. He did his original artwork in black and white. All the color that was later added was done by hand.

Mai Vo-Dinh *pages 38–41*

Mai Vo-Dinh vividly remembers his childhood in Vietnam and the pleasure he took in hearing folk tales told aloud. He has lived and worked in the United States since 1960, and became a citizen in 1976. This author also illustrates books. His oil paintings and woodcuts have been displayed in museums and art galleries.

Books &

More by Lewis Carroll

Jabberwocky
illustrated by Jane Zalbin
This wonderful nonsense poem is enhanced by detailed illustrations.

Through the Looking Glass & What Alice Found There
illustrated by John Tenniel
In this sequel, Alice visits a land where she becomes a pawn in an absurd game of chess and meets all sorts of funny characters.

Johnny Tremain
by Esther Forbes
In this classic novel about the Sons of Liberty, Johnny is falsely accused of a crime. Will he be able to prove his innocence when his case goes to trial?

Nothing but the Truth
by Avi
There is more than one side to every story, even if everyone maintains that he or she is telling "nothing but the truth."

Roll of Thunder, Hear My Cry
by Mildred D. Taylor
Cassie Logan and her family never lose sight of what is rightfully theirs—even when others try to deny them their rights.

Hand, Heart, Mind: The Story of the Education of America's Deaf People
by Lou Ann Walker
For over a hundred years, deaf people have been engaged in a civil rights struggle. This is the fascinating story of the triumphs and setbacks of the movement to achieve equal educational opportunities for deaf people.

Hiawatha: Messenger of Peace
by Dennis Bindell Fraden
This Iroquois leader found a way to unite warring tribes into the Iroquois Confederacy. The Confederacy of states that Hiawatha founded worked so well that Benjamin Franklin and others studied the Iroquois system when creating our own United States.

×Media

Videos

The Ernest Green Story
Disney
It's 1957 in Little Rock, Arkansas, where there are two high schools: Horace Mann and Central. Central is for white students only. But the laws have just changed and Ernie Green is an African-American student allowed to attend Central. Here is the true story of how one young man made a difference. (65 minutes)

Frog Girl: The Jennifer Graham Story
by David Eagle
This is the true story of a tenth grader who asked to be excused from dissecting a frog in class and ended up in a court hearing. (47 minutes)

Sunrise at Campobello
Warner
Franklin D. Roosevelt was a young man when he got polio, but he went on to become President of the U.S. (115 minutes)

Software

Capitol Hill
Software Toolworks
(Macintosh, IBM, MPC)
Experience being a member of Congress with this interactive CD-ROM program.

Origins of the Constitution
Queue
(Macintosh, IBM/CD-ROM)
Explore the personalities and philosophies that went into the making of this historic document.

Timeliner Data Disk: Women in History
Tom Snyder
(Apple, Macintosh, IBM)
Used in conjunction with the basic Timeliner software, this resource allows you to create time lines and documents about the role of women and their accomplishments throughout history.

Magazines

Cobblestone: The History Magazine for Young People
Cobblestone Publishing
Throughout history the search for justice has inspired positive change. Each issue of this theme-related magazine focuses on a different topic.

Scholastic News
Scholastic Inc.
This current events magazine is full of interesting information about government and many other aspects of contemporary life.

A Place to Write

**National Forensic League
671 Fond du Lac
Ripon, WI 54971**

One forum for expressing your views is public debate. Contact the National Forensic League if you're interested in public speaking, debate, and discussion.

Acknowledgments

Grateful acknowledgment is made to the following sources for permission to reprint from previously published material. The publisher has made diligent efforts to trace the ownership of all copyrighted material in this volume and believes that all necessary permissions have been secured. If any errors or omissions have inadvertently been made, proper corrections will gladly be made in future editions.

Cover: 10-K WALK is a reproduction of an oil on canvas painting by Synthia Saint James. Copyright © 1992. All rights reserved. Used by permission of the artist.

Interior: Selections and cover from YOU BE THE JURY: COURTROOM III by Marvin Miller. Copyright © 1990 by Marvin Miller. Cover illustration by Bob Roper. Reprinted by permission of Scholastic Inc.

"Martha Washington," "Future Farmers of America," "Amelia Earhart," "International Red Cross," "Wildlife Conservation/Whooping Crane," "100 Years of Progress of Women," "U.S. Man in Space/Project Mercury," "200th Anniversary-Birth of Betsy Ross," "Forest Conservation," "Abe Lincoln," "Water Conservation," "Founder of American Red Cross-Clara Barton," "Lafayette 1757-1957," "Founder of the Girl Scouts," and "The American Woman" Stamp Designs copyright © United States Postal Service. All rights reserved.

"The Wisdom of Solomon" from the DOUBLEDAY ILLUSTRATED CHILDREN'S BIBLE by Sandol Stoddard. Copyright © 1983 by Nelson Doubleday, Inc. Reprinted by arrangement with GuildAmerica Books, an imprint of Doubleday Books & Music Clubs, Inc.

"The Fly" from THE TOAD IS THE EMPEROR'S UNCLE, ANIMAL FOLKTALES FROM VIETNAM by Mai Vo-Dinh. Copyright © 1970 by Mai Vo-Dinh. Used by permission of the author.

"The Stone in the Temple" by Aaron Shepard. Copyright © 1995 by Aaron Shepard. First appeared in Cricket Magazine, June 1995. Reprinted by permission of the author.

Selections from California Vehicle Code §21212 Youth Bicycle Helmets: Minors (pp. 611-612).

"The Rebellious Alphabet" and cover from THE REBELLIOUS ALPHABET by Jorge Diaz, illustrated by Øivind S. Jorfald. Translation copyright © 1993 by Geoffrey Fox/text copyright © 1977 by Jorge Diaz. Illustrations copyright © 1992 by Øivind S. Jorfald. Reprinted by arrangement with Henry Holt and Co.

Selections from HEADLINES: REAL BUT RIDICULOUS SAMPLINGS FROM AMERICA'S NEWSPAPERS compiled by Jay Leno. Copyright © 1989 by Big Dog Productions, Inc. Reprinted by permission of Warner Books, Inc.

Selection from DATELINE AMERICA by Charles Kuralt. Copyright © 1989 by CBS Inc. Reprinted by permission of Harcourt Brace & Company.

The CBS Radio Network and "Eye" logo is a service mark of CBS Inc. and is used by permission.

"Tools for Change" and cover from IT'S OUR WORLD, TOO! by Phillip Hoose, cover photographs by Harold Feinstein. Copyright © 1993 by Phillip Hoose. Reprinted by permission of Little, Brown and Company.

"Honoring Their Ancestors" and cover from KIDS WITH COURAGE: TRUE STORIES ABOUT YOUNG PEOPLE MAKING A DIFFERENCE by Barbara A. Lewis. Copyright © 1992 by Barbara A. Lewis. Reprinted with permission of Free Spirit Publishing Inc., Minneapolis, MN. All rights reserved. Cover photos courtesy of the Ute Bulletin.

"Point/Counterpoint Chart" adapted from "Are Tests a Good Measure of What You Have Learned?" from Scholastic Action Magazine, January 15, 1993. Copyright © 1993 by Scholastic Inc. Special thanks to Ms. Marsha Stoddard's class at Northeast High in Meridian, MS, for participating in the debate.

Selection and cover from SHILOH by Phyllis Reynolds Naylor. Text copyright © 1991 by Phyllis Reynolds Naylor, reprinted by permission of Atheneum Books for Young Readers, an imprint of Simon & Schuster Children's Publishing Division. Cover illustration copyright © 1991 by Dell Publishing, used by permission of Dell Books, a division of Bantam Doubleday Dell Publishing Group, Inc.

"If I Were in Charge of the World" and cover from IF I WERE IN CHARGE OF THE WORLD AND OTHER WORRIES by Judith Viorst, illustrated by Lynne Cherry. Text copyright © 1981 by Judith Viorst. Cover illustration copyright © 1981 by Lynne Cherry. Reprinted by permission of Atheneum Books for Young Readers, an imprint of Simon & Schuster.

Selections from ELEANOR ROOSEVELT: A LIFE OF DISCOVERY by Russell Freedman. Text copyright © 1993 by Russell Freedman. Reprinted by permission of Clarion Books, a Houghton Mifflin Company imprint. All rights reserved.

"The Universal Declaration of Human Rights" from the United Nations.

"Nelson Mandela: Champion of Freedom" by Carol Gelber from FACES: The Magazine About People, January 1991 issue: South Africa. Copyright © 1991 Cobblestone Publishing, Inc., 7 School St., Peterborough, NH 03458. Reprinted by permission of the publisher.

South Africa at a Glance adapted from "A Land in Flux" by Phil Sudo from Scholastic Update, February 25, 1994. Copyright © 1994 by Scholastic Inc.

Cover from THE DAY THE WOMEN GOT THE VOTE: A PHOTO HISTORY OF THE WOMEN'S RIGHTS MOVEMENT by George Sullivan. Top right: March in support of the ERA, Washington, DC, 1977—Washington Star Collection, Martin Luther King Library. Clockwise from middle left: World War II WACs—National Archives; A woman working in an area formerly closed to women—AP/Wide World; Jackie Joyner Kersee displays the second gold medal she won in the 1988 Olympic Games—AP/Wide World; Eleanor Roosevelt, May 14, 1958—UPI/Bettman; Susan B. Anthony—AP/Wide World. Published by Scholastic Inc.

Cover from NELSON MANDELA: "NO EASY WALK TO FREEDOM" by Barry Denenberg, photo by Luis Grubb/JB Pictures. Published by Scholastic Inc.

Cover from THURGOOD MARSHALL: CHAMPION OF JUSTICE by G. S. Prentzas. Cover illustration by Daniel Mark Duffy, copyright © 1994 by Chelsea House Publishers, a division of Main Line Book Company. Published by Chelsea House Publishers, a division of Main Line Book Company.

Cover from THE TRUE CONFESSIONS OF CHARLOTTE DOYLE by Avi. Cover illustration by Ruth E. Murray, copyright © 1990 by Ruth E. Murray. Published by Orchard Books.

Photography and Illustration Credits

Selection Openers: Greg Couch.

Photos: All Tools in Workshops and Projects © John Lei for Scholastic Inc. unless otherwise noted. p. 2 bl: © Jackson Hill for Scholastic Inc. pp. 2-3 background: © Jackson Hill/Southern Lights Photography, Inc.; ml: © Jackson Hill for Scholastic Inc.; tl: © Jackson Hill for Scholastic Inc. p. 3 bc: © Jackson Hill for Scholastic Inc.; tc: © Telegraph Colour Library/FPG International Corp. p. 4 c: © Jackson Hill for Scholastic Inc.; tc: © Telegraph Colour Library/FPG International Corp. p. 5 c: © E. Alan McGee/FPG International Corp.; tc: © Telegraph Colour Library/FPG International Corp. p. 6 c: © Francis Clark Westfield for Scholastic Inc.; tc: © Telegraph Colour Library/FPG International Corp. pp. 32-33 c: © Jackson Hill for Scholastic Inc. p. 32 bl, ml, tl, tr: © Jackson Hill for Scholastic Inc.; tc: © Telegraph Colour Library/FPG International Corp. p. 33: © Jackson Hill for Scholastic Inc. p. 34 bc, bl, tl: © Jackson Hill for Scholastic Inc.; mr: © Jackson Hill/Southern Lights Photography, Inc. p. 35 mr: © Jackson Hill for Scholastic Inc. p. 44 bc: © Stanley Bach for Scholastic Inc. p. 46 bl: © Lori Adamski Peek/Tony Stone Images. p. 47 bc: © Stanley Bach for Scholastic Inc.; br: Jackson Hill for Scholastic Inc. p. 63 bl, mr, tl: © Joseph Del Valle, courtesy NBC Studios. p. 65 bc: © The Granger Collection. p. 67 br: © Stephen Ogilvy for Scholastic Inc. p. 68 br: © Stephen Ogilvy for Scholastic Inc. p. 71 br: © Stephen Ogilvy for Scholastic Inc. p. 73 br: © Stephen Ogilvy for Scholastic Inc. p. 75 bc: © Stephen Ogilvy for Scholastic Inc. p. 76 c: © Stephen Trimble. p. 81 bl, br: © Stephen Trimble. p. 83 tc: © Free Spirit Publishing. pp. 86-87 br: © Stanley Bach for Scholastic Inc. pp. 88-89 mr: © W. Woodworth/SuperStock, Inc. p. 88 bl: © Stanley Bach for Scholastic Inc.; c: © Gay Bumgarner/Tony Stone Images. p. 89 bl: © Stanley Bach for Scholastic Inc.; br: © Jackson Hill for Scholastic Inc. p. 106 bl: © Francis Clark Westfield for Scholastic Inc. p. 108 c: Courtesy Franklin Delano Roosevelt Library. p. 109 tc: The Bettmann Archive. pp. 111-117 all photographs: Courtesy Franklin Delano Roosevelt Library. p. 120 c: © Eric Bouvey/The Gamma Liaison Network. p. 122 ml: © Owen P.D./Black Star. p. 123 mr: © Ken Oosterbroek/The Gamma Liaison Network. p. 124 mr: © Mark Reinstein/The Gamma Liaison Network. p. 125 c: © Ken Oosterbroek/The Gamma Liaison Network. p. 126 c: © Garth Lumley/The Gamma Liaison Network. p. 127 bl: © Selwyn Tait/The Gamma Liaison Network; tl: © Reuters/The Bettmann Archive. pp. 130-131 c: © Stanley Bach for Scholastic Inc. p. 132 c: © Stanley Bach for Scholastic Inc.; mr: © Keith Wood/Tony Stone Images. p. 133 bc: © Rivera Collection/SuperStock, Inc.; ml: © R. Heinzen/SuperStock, Inc. p. 134 bc: © Stanley Bach for Scholastic Inc. p. 135 bl: © Stanley Bach for Scholastic Inc.; br: © Jackson Hill for Scholastic Inc. p. 136 bc: © David Michael Davis/FPG International Corp. p. 137 mr: © Russ Kinne/Comstock Inc. p. 138 tr: © Ron Chapple/FPG International Corp. p. 139 bc: © Markel/Gamma Liaison International. p. 140 bl: © Charles Osgood; tl: © The Bettmann Archive. p. 141 br: © Courtesy of Mai Vo-Dinh; mr: The Bettmann Archive; tr: UPI/ The Bettmann Archive. p. 143 br: © Stephen Ogilvy for Scholastic Inc.

Illustrations: Section Openers: Ed Tadiello; p. 24: Wendell Minor; pp. 26, 30, 31: Amy Wasserman; pp. 36, 41, 42-43: Maria Korusiewicz; pp. 30, 35: David Diaz.